VINTAGE
LIVING
TEXTS

THE ESSENTIAL
GUIDE TO
CONTEMPORARY
LITERATURE

Iris Murdoch

SERIES EDITORS
Jonathan Noakes
and
Margaret Reynolds
with Louisa Joyner

Also available in Vintage Living Texts

'An excellent and timely series, very useful for students, well-produced and well-written.'
Dr Robert Eaglestone, Royal Holloway,
University of London

'I am impressed. Students will find these texts extremely useful, and serious general readers, too.'
Professor Chris Woodhead, former Chief Inspector of Schools

'Margaret Reynolds and Jonathan Noakes are at the cutting edge of providing English teachers with the support they need for teaching the contemporary novel.'
Dr Vivian Anthony, Training Co-ordinator, Professional Development Services for HMC schools

'Two highly sensitive and intelligent teachers (from school and university) lead us into dialogue with the author, the texts and their context and help us to question what and how we are reading and to arrive at illuminating answers. Such dialogue is the essence of good practice in teaching literature.'
John Venning, Head of English,
St Paul's School for Boys, London

'This series is the first to teach students what they most need to learn: how to teach themselves. It is informative, rigorous and yet, more importantly, playful. It combines the qualities of the best teaching.'
Anthea Church, Head of English, Kent College, Pembury

VINTAGE
LIVING
TEXTS

Iris Murdoch

THE ESSENTIAL GUIDE
TO CONTEMPORARY
LITERATURE

The Bell
The Black Prince
The Sea, The Sea

VINTAGE

Published by Vintage 2004

2 4 6 8 10 9 7 5 3 1

Copyright © Jonathan Noakes and Margaret Reynolds 2003

The right of Jonathan Noakes and Margaret Reynolds to be identified as the authors of this work has been asserted by them in accordance with the Copyright, Designs and Patents Act, 1988.

First published in Great Britain in 2004 by Vintage
Random House, 20 Vauxhall Bridge Road,
London SW1V 2SA

Random House Australia (Pty) Limited
20 Alfred Street, Milsons Point, Sydney,
New South Wales 2061, Australia

Random House New Zealand Limited
18 Poland Road, Glenfield,
Auckland 10, New Zealand

Random House (Pty) Limited
Endulini, 5A Jubilee Road, Parktown 2193, South Africa

The Random House Group Limited Reg. No. 954009
www.randomhouse.co.uk

A CIP catalogue record for this book is available from the British Library

ISBN 0 099 452227

Papers used by Random House are natural, recyclable products made from wood grown in sustainable forests; the manufacturing processes conform to the environmental regulations of the country of origin.

Typeset by Palimpsest Book Production Limited, Polmont, Stirlingshire

Printed and bound in Great Britain by
Bookmarque Ltd, Croydon, Surrey

While every effort has been made to obtain permission from owners of copyright material reproduced herein, the publishers would like to apologise for any omissions and will be pleased to incorporate missing acknowledgements in any future editions.

CONTENTS

The Sea, The Sea

VINTAGE LIVING TEXTS: REFERENCE

Acknowledgements

We owe grateful thanks to all at Random House. Most of all our debt is to Rachel Cugnoni and her team at Vintage – especially to Ali Reynolds – Jason Arthur, Liz Foley, Katherine Fry and Jack Murphy who have given us generous and unfailing support. Thanks also to Caroline Michel, Marcella Edwards, Philippa Brewster and Georgina Capel, Michael Meredith, Angela Leighton, Harriet Marland, to all our colleagues and friends, and to our partners and families. We would also like to thank the teachers and students at schools and colleges around the country who have taken part in our trialling process, and who have responded so readily and warmly to our requests for advice.

VINTAGE LIVING TEXTS

Preface

About this series

Vintage Living Texts: The Essential Guide to Contemporary Literature is a new concept in reading guides. Our aim is to provide readers of all kinds with an intelligent and accessible introduction to key works of contemporary literature. Each guide suggests techniques for reading important contemporary novels, and offers a variety of back-up materials that will give you ways into the text – without ever telling you what to think.

Content

Usually the books reproduce an extensive interview with the author, conducted exclusively for this series. This is not to say that we believe that the author's word is law. Of course it isn't. Once his or her book has gone out into the world he or she becomes simply yet another – if singularly competent – reader. This series recognises that an author's contribution may be valuable, and intriguing, but it puts the reader in control. In the case of *Iris Murdoch* we have included an account drawn from published interviews with, or prefaces by, Iris Murdoch to offer perspectives on her literary opinions, methods and preoccupations. Most of the titles in the series are author-focused and cover at least three novels by that writer, along with relevant biographical, bibliographical, contextual and comparative material. With *Iris Murdoch* we are catering for a particular school and college audience who often study these three key works of twentieth-century fiction.

How to use this series

In the reading activities that make up the core of each book you will see that you are asked to do two things. One comes from the text; that is, we suggest what you should focus on, whether it's a theme, the language or the narrative method. The other concentrates on your own response. We want you to think about how you are reading and what skills you are bringing to bear in doing that reading. So this part is very much about you, the reader.

The point is that there are many ways of responding to a text. You could concentrate on the methods you might use to compare this text with others. In that case, look for the sections headed 'Compare'. Or you might want to do something more individual, and analyse how you are reacting to a text and what it means to you, in which case, pick out the approaches labelled 'Imagine' or 'Ask Yourself'.

Of course, it may well be that you are reading these texts for an examination. In that case you will have to go for the more traditional methods of literary criticism and look for the responses that tell you to 'Discuss' or 'Analyse'. Whichever level you (or your students) are at, you will find that there is something here for everyone. However, we're not suggesting that you stick solely to the approaches we offer, or that you tackle all of the exercises laid out here. Choose whatever most interests you, or whatever best suits your purposes.

Who are these books for?

Students will find that these guides are like a good teacher. They introduce the life and work of the author, set each novel in its context, explain key ideas and literary critical terms as they arise, suggest comparative exercises in a number of media, and ask focused questions to encourage a well-informed, analytical approach to reading the novels in a way that is rigorous, but still entertaining.

Teachers will find in this series a rich source of ideas for teaching contemporary novels and their contexts, particularly at AS, A and undergraduate levels. The exercises on each text have been tailored to meet the various assessment objectives laid down in the subject criteria for GCE AS and GCE A Level and the International Baccalaureate in English Literature, and are explained in such a way that they can easily be selected and fitted into a lesson plan. Given the diversity of ways in which the awarding bodies have devised their specifications to meet these assessment objectives, a wide range of exercises is offered. We've had fun devising the plans, and we hope they'll be fun for you when you come to teach and learn with them.

And if you are neither a teacher nor a student of contemporary literature, but someone reading for your own pleasure? Well, if you've ever wanted someone to introduce you to a novelist's work in a way that will let you trust your own judgement and read more confidently, then this guide is also for you.

Whoever you are, we hope that you will enjoy using these books and that they will send you back to the novels to find new pleasures.

All page references to *The Bell*, *The Black Prince* and *The Sea, The Sea* in this text refer to the Vintage editions.

Iris Murdoch

Introduction

Of all the novelists working in the second half of the twentieth century, Iris Murdoch has occupied the most peculiar position. Though she produced some twenty-six novels from 1954 to 1995 we are now tempted to wonder whether she can simply be classed as 'a novelist' at all. While turning out these remarkable works of fiction, Murdoch taught philosophy in an intense and demanding academic position as a Fellow of St Anne's at Oxford, consistently writing elegant, complicated and profound works in her professional capacity. It may be that – in spite of the characters, the plots, the structures, the symbolism, the narrative styles – Murdoch's fictional works can also be read as works of philosophy.

Murdoch's own remarks on the subject suggest that, while her fictional works drew on her philosophical expertise, they were not to be confused with 'real' philosophy. As she once explained:

> I am a teacher of philosophy and I am trained as a philosopher and I 'do' philosophy and I teach philosophy, but philosophy is fantastically difficult and I

think those who attempt to write it would probably agree that there are very few moments when they rise to the level of real philosophy. One is writing about philosophy . . . One is not actually doing the real thing.

Nevertheless, in some ways all Murdoch's novels deal with the same problem (a problem also discussed at length in her academic work): how can human beings, who crave the consolation of order, come to terms with a lack of pattern in a haphazard universe? This is the question in her 1961 essay 'Against Dryness'; it appears also in 'The Sublime and the Good' (1959), and in the much later *Metaphysics as a Guide to Morals* (published in 1992). It is also a recurring question tackled within her novels. In many ways this explains why Murdoch was such a prolific writer; she was always seeking an answer to her question. But, by definition, in the process of putting it into a novel shape, by squeezing this oozing world into a lengthy novel, she inevitably did create an order. The only way to resist that order was to start again with nothing, with the blank page where – yet again – she would try to replicate accident, contingency, chaos, chance and all the haphazard variables in her view of the world.

The drive to shape, pattern and define destiny is overwhelming, in life, and most certainly in fiction. In *The Bell* her structuring devices consist of the symbol of the bell itself, or the contrast set up between town and country. In *The Black Prince* a structure is centred around Bradley's narrative method, his delay and digression, and his neat mirroring of the opening scene at the ending of the novel. In *The Sea, The Sea* it is Charles's obsessive account of his meals, or his habit of thumbing through past loves, that affords the novel a comic shape. And yet in each work there are surprises and gratuitous accidents to remind us of the frailty of our human condition and the indifference of a universe which is always changeable and unpredictable.

As a philosopher and academic Murdoch cared about getting things right, and especially about expressing ideas rightly. In her introduction to the Vintage edition of *The Black Prince*, the writer Candia McWilliam speaks of her own childish memory of an overheard criticism of Murdoch's writing. This unidentified adult critic had said that they wished Iris Murdoch would not 'write her adjectives in threes'.

Once you are aware of this pattern, you can't help noticing it. McWilliam decides that this is fine, that this trait in Murdoch's writing indicates 'a want of perfectedness'. Further – and importantly – McWilliam decides that this 'want of perfectedness' is 'holy' to the 'artist and philosopher' in Murdoch. The piles of adjectives suggest a reaching after, a striving, a 'raggedness' (McWilliam's word) that explores and deplores and applauds and admires the inevitable human failure to make things perfect while – at exactly the same time – it admires and applauds the intense human desire to make things perfect. Murdoch's provisional writing style imitates what she saw as our inescapably provisional way of life.

Being a philosopher, this was a paradox which Murdoch faced clear-eyed and undismayed. As she wrote in *The Sovereignty of Good*:

> I can see no evidence to suggest that human life is not something self-contained. There are properly many patterns and purposes within life, but there is no general and as it were externally guaranteed pattern or purpose of the kind for which philosophers and theologians used to search. We are what we seem to be, transient mortal creatures subject to change . . . Our destiny can be examined, but it cannot be justified or totally explained. We are simply here.

We may be 'simply here', but the simpleness of being here means that Murdoch – and her characters – go on giving us gems along the way. Here are two examples of her 'self-contained' view of life, taken from *The Black Prince*. The first (p. 232) is about consciousness and the circadian clock that regulates our physical lives:

> The division of one day from the next must be one of the most profound peculiarities of life on this planet. It is, on the whole, a merciful arrangement. We are not condemned to sustained flights of being, but are constantly refreshed by little holidays from ourselves. We are intermittent creatures, always falling to little ends and rising to little beginnings. Our soon-tired consciousness is meted out in chapters, and that the world will look quite different tomorrow is, both for our comfort and our discomfort, usually true.

And the second (p. 316) is about the strange precision of desire:

> The absolute yearning of one human body for another particular one and its indifference to substitutes is one of life's major mysteries.

It is, of course, the character of Bradley Pearson who offers these profound words. He is arrogant, self-absorbed, vain, pedantic and pathetic. But – because he is Murdoch's creation – he is also wise, if only intermittently and accidentally.

Murdoch herself has become something of a heroine in recent times. This is largely due, first of all, to her husband John Bayley's memoir, *Iris*, which described the sad mental decline of her last years. In addition, it is due to the film *Iris* directed by Richard Eyre and starring Kate Winslet as the young author and Judi Dench who played her in old age. Peter Conradi has also written the definitive biography of Murdoch and his important 1986 critical work has been reissued as *The Saint and the Artist*. In addition, A. S. Byatt's magisterial and pioneering work on Murdoch, *Degrees of Freedom* – first published in 1965 – has also been reissued.

The best understanding of Murdoch is, of course, gleaned from her novels. If her fiction acknowledges the provisional and refuses to console, it is nonetheless optimistic because Murdoch cared about people. It is her own love affair with human beings and with all things 'human' that comes across so strongly in all her works. In her early essay 'The Sublime and the Good', Murdoch wrote:

> Love is the extremely difficult realisation that some-thing other than oneself is real. Love, and so art and morals, is the discovery of reality. What stuns us into the realisation of our super sensible destiny is not, as Kant imagined, the formlessness of nature, but rather its unutterable particularity; and the most particular and individual of all things is the mind of man.

Murdoch puts her characters through crises in which they are forced to think and to examine their lives. It is the whole point of living an examined life – there will never be one answer, there will never be a solution, or a conclusion. Just as Murdoch so often used three adjectives to arrive at some exactitude, so she had to go on with her questing with a vast number of novels. But every so often there will be a revelation which will seem to define all you need to know, and which demonstrates the power and achievement within Murdoch's work.

Interviews and Silences

All the *Vintage Living Texts* reading guides include, where possible, an interview with the author featured. In the case of this guide to three novels by Murdoch we cannot speak directly to the author who died in 1999. During her lifetime, however, Murdoch gave many interviews, some to journalists, but also to academics and critics. You will find a list of some of these interviews in the Select Bibliography. In addition, Murdoch also wrote many academic and philosophical articles and books.

Instead of a conventional interview, we have constructed a patchwork to provide a sense of Murdoch's 'voice', relating to the three novels in focus. We have devised the questions that we would have liked to ask Murdoch and the answers that you find given here are Murdoch's own and in her own words. The first section draws on the interview which she gave to John Haffenden and which was published in his book *Novelists in Interview* (1985). Page references to this edition are given after each 'answer' taken from that source. Other 'answers' are quotations taken from various of Murdoch's critical works. Again, full references follow the 'answer'.

This question-and-answer format is designed to help you think about how you might use interviews and works by an author as a critical resource. You may find that this is a useful method to adopt in considering your own reading of other writers' published 'introductions' to their own work.

QUESTION: So many of your works draw on minute descriptions of places and settings, landscapes and colours. How important is the precision of setting to you?

IM: At one time I wanted to be a painter. I think I would have been a moderate painter if I had given my life to it, but that is an absolute hypothesis without any basis to it! I do sometimes try to paint, but I haven't got any training. So this is just a dream life. I envy painters, I think they are happy people. The painter lives with his craft the whole time: the visual world, which I adore, is always present, and the artist can always be thinking about his work, being inspired by light and so on. Painters can have a nice time.
Novelists in Interview (p. 199).

QUESTION: It seems that you care very deeply about people, and about how human beings live their lives. Is that a reasonable element to consider in terms of your work?

IM: It begins with an interest in human beings, but any writer is inevitably going to work with his own anxieties and desires. If the book is any good it has got to have in it the fire of a personal unconscious mind.
Novelists in Interview (p. 198)

QUESTION: How does Shakespeare's *The Tempest* connect to your own novel *The Sea, The Sea*?

IM: I've always got *The Tempest* in my head . . . the idea of giving up magic, the relation between religion and power, and so on. John Robert [in *The Philosopher's Pupil* and also Charles

Arrowby in *The Sea, The Sea*] is a power figure, he can't help exercising power . . . But don't overdo *The Tempest* here [in association with *The Philosopher's Pupil*], because the relation to *The Tempest* is terribly shadowy . . . *The Tempest* is very deeply in my mind, but it's not what the book is about. The book is about what it's about.
Novelists in Interview (pp. 195 and 198)

QUESTION: Why are you so interested in the imagery associated with water?

IM: There is water in all the books. Thinking of the background to the drowning [of John Robert in *The Philosopher's Pupil*], one image printed on my mind is from a film that I saw a hundred years ago, *Les Enfants du Paradis*, where there is a murder in a swimming bath (though the character in the film is not drowned but shot, I think). When I was in China I visited a bath establishment, which also struck my imagination, and in Iceland I have been in warm pools where it is great to swim on a cold day. I do love swimming. I used to be absolutely fearless in the sea, but I nearly drowned once, and I'm now much more cautious. I used to think the sea and I were great friends, but one must fear the sea.
Novelists in Interview (p. 197)

QUESTION: So much of what goes on in *The Sea, The Sea* concerns Charles Arrowby's reliving – and rewriting – of his own past and his own obsessions. What do you feel is significant about the past and about obsessing over our hidden pasts?

IM: It's a salient thing in human life, one of the most general features of human beings, that they may be dominated by remorse or by some plan of their lives which may have gone wrong. I think it's one of the things that prevents people from

13

being good. Why are people not good, and why, without being evil or even having bad intentions, do they do bad things? Schopenhauer, whom I admire, is good on this topic of tragedy. Some people who are not bad find themselves so situated that they are unable to stop themselves from doing the greatest possible harm they can to others. It is an evident feature of human psychology that people have secret dream lives. The secrecy of people is very interesting, and the novelist is overcoming the secrecy and attempting to understand. Readers sometimes say to me that I portray odd characters; but the secret thoughts and obsessions and fantasies of others would amaze one, only people don't tell them, partly because they're ashamed and partly because secrecy is very natural and proper. *Novelists in Interview* (pp. 201–2)

QUESTION: How far do you see your novels as sharing themes or methods? In what ways might all of your fiction be connected?

IM: I find myself thinking in terms of two kinds of novel which might be called 'open' and 'closed', and I cannot at the moment decide which kind I want to write: perhaps, more or less alternately, both. The open novel contains a lot of characters who rush about independently, each one eccentric and self-centred; the plot to some extent situates them in a pattern but does not integrate them into a single system. The closed novel has fewer characters and tends to draw them, as it were, toward a single point. *Under the Net* and *The Flight from the Enchanter* were, I think, ['closed'], *The Sandcastle* and *The Bell* [were 'open']. The advantage of the open novel is that it is bright and airy and the characters move about freely; it is more like life as it is normally lived. Its disadvantage is that it may become loose in texture and it is more difficult to make the structure evident. A closed novel is more intensely integrated but may be more

14

claustrophobic in atmosphere and the characters may lose their sense of freedom. Ideally, and if one were a great writer, one could, I think, combine both these things in a single work and not have to oscillate between them.

Interviewed in *The Bookman* (November 1958), p. 26

QUESTION: So many of your books address the question of virtue or 'goodness'. It is in *The Black Prince* and, to a lesser degree, in *The Sea, The Sea*. How do you conceive of 'goodness' and how can it be realised in the world?

IM: Virtue is not essentially or immediately concerned with choosing between actions, or rules or reasons, nor with stripping the personality for a leap. It is concerned with really apprehending that other people exist. This too is what freedom really is; and it is impossible not to feel the creation of a work of art as a struggle for freedom. Freedom is not choosing; that is merely the move we make when all is already lost. Freedom is knowing and understanding and respecting things quite other than ourselves. Virtue is in this sense to be construed as knowledge, and connects us with reality . . . The artist is indeed the analogon of the good man, and in a special sense he is the good man: the lover who, nothing himself, lets others be through him.

'The Sublime and the Beautiful Revisited', in the *Yale Review*, Vol. 49 (pp. 269–70)

QUESTION: Another of your key subjects is love, both its effects and its terrors. But you are also concerned with defining love. Outside the definitions provided in your fictions, what would you say love is?

IM: Art and morality are, with certain provisos . . . one. Their essence is the same. The essence of both of them is love. Love is the perception of individuals. Love is the extremely difficult realisation that something other than oneself is real. Love, and so art and morals, is the discovery of reality.

'The Sublime and the Good', in *Existentialists and Mystics: Writings on Philosophy and Literature* (p. 215)

QUESTION: What, in your view, are the 'uses' of literature in life?

IM: Through literature we can rediscover a sense of the density of our lives. Literature can help us to recover from the ailments of Romanticism. If it can be said to have a task, now, that surely is its task. But if it is to perform it, prose must recover its former glory, eloquence and discourse must return. I would connect eloquence with the attempt to speak the truth.

'Against Dryness', *Encounter*, no. 88, January 1961 (p. 20)

There is a sort of pedagogue in my novels. I think a novelist must be truthful. Bad novels project various personal daydreams – the daydream of power, for example, or of being fearfully sexually attractive and so on – and this can be horrid. But the contingent nature of life and what human failings are like, and also what it's like for somebody to be good: all this is very difficult, and it's where truthfulness comes in, to stop yourself from telling something which is a lie.

Novelists in Interview (p. 205)

VINTAGE
LIVING
TEXTS

The Bell

IN CLOSE-UP

Reading guides for

THE BELL

BEFORE YOU BEGIN TO READ . . .

— Read the introduction and the section in this book entitled Interviews and Silences. From these you will be able to identify a number of themes that are discussed in *The Bell*. These themes might include:

- The power of mythology
- The idea of community
- The image of the bell

Other themes that may be useful to consider while reading the novel include:

- Ownership
- Men and women
- Past and present

Reading activities: detailed analysis

CHAPTER I
(pp. 7–25)

Focus on: openings

ANALYSE . . .

— 'Dora Greenfield left her husband because she was afraid of him. She decided six months later to return to him for the same reason' (p. 7). Stop and examine the opening sentences of this novel. Think about the expectations that they set up for the reader. For example: who is speaking? who is 'Dora'?

— Work your way through the opening paragraph, drawing up a list of the expectations that are created here and focusing on the issues that you expect the novel to raise and resolve.

— When you have drawn up a comprehensive list, turn to the rest of this opening section. How many of your questions are answered here? Is the reader told who is speaking? Does this opening section of the novel tell us more about Dora and Paul's relationship?

COMPARE . . .

— Look over your questions and the evidence you have gleaned from the text. Which questions still remain unanswered? How comprehensive are the answers you have managed to establish? Compare the questions which do not yet have answers with those that you have found textual evidence for. Are there any themes that link the unanswered questions together?

DISCUSS . . .

— Using the questions, answers and comparisons you have worked on, think about how the opening sentences establish the themes of the novel. When you have arrived at some answers working alone, compare the questions and answers you have come up with with other people's conclusions. Have you and your friends identified the same themes through your close readings?

— Think about the questions your analysis has provided. Are these 'mysteries'? How does the information Murdoch refuses to give you make the text difficult to read, or 'mysterious'? Or, do the unanswered questions help to create readers' expectations? Do we read the novel looking for particular information, or clues?

EXAMINE AND EVALUATE . . .

— As you work your way through the novel keep an eye on your questions – are they ever answered? If so, at what point in the text are you given this textual evidence? What difference does it make to the novel *when* information is given, or for how long it has been withheld? Are there any questions that remain unanswered? In what ways do they influence your interpretation of the novel?

— As you become more familiar with the novel, think also about how Murdoch *subverts* your expectations. To what extent is the focus of the opening chapter also the focus of the novel as a whole? Think particularly about:

- Characters
- Setting
- Themes
- Relationships

— Use the categories above to break down your analysis. Are the themes and characters introduced in Chapter 1 the novel's main concern?

CHAPTER 2
(pp. 26–39)

Focus on: town versus country

PICK OUT . . .
— Work your way through this chapter thinking about which character Murdoch is aligning us with. Which of these journeys are you most interested and involved in – Dora's journey from the town to the country, or Paul's decision to come and collect his disobedient wife from the station? Think carefully about your choice. How does Murdoch direct your attention? What words and phrases does she employ in order to gain your sympathy?

DEVELOP . . .
— When you have thought closely about the different journeys accounted for here, explore the idea of the journey as a metaphor for emotional, psychological and intellectual development. How is Toby's journey represented here? How do these different journeys influence your expectations for the novel as a whole?

Focus on: institutions

QUESTION AND INTERROGATE . . .

— What is an institution? You might want to look up the word in a dictionary to give yourself a starting point. To what extent would you agree with the definition you have found? How, for example, would you categorise the following list – are some/all of them 'institutions'? Be careful to justify your choices.

- A school
- A hospital
- A church
- The doctrines of the Catholic Church
- A nightclub
- A prison
- A television programme (e.g. *EastEnders*, *Coronation Street*)
- Marriage

EXPLORE . . .

— To what extent is your life *circumscribed* by institutions? Do you regard institutions positively – do they serve to protect people? Or do you think of them, rather, as an infringement of your right to individual choice? Consider the positive and negative connotations of an institution, and how each type of institution can affect individual people.

DISCUSS . . .

— Discuss with other readers the choices you have made in deciding whether or not the items in the above list are 'institutions'. What differences do you note in your definitions? How does this challenge your understanding of the term 'institution'?

RETURN . . .

— Now turn your attention back to the novel. To what extent are Toby and Dora entering an 'institution'? Through your analysis, you have constructed a working definition of what you understand an institution to be – to what extent does Imber fit your model? Remember to draw evidence from the text itself to support your view. You may want to get into pairs for this task, working through your differing interpretations of the term.

CHAPTER 3
(pp. 40–5)

Focus on: storytelling

DETAIL . . .

— Take your time working through this chapter and note closely the myth you are given here. Who does it feature? Who is the narrator? Who is the audience – who is being spoken to directly? Do you have the same reaction to the story as the audience who are present in the novel?

CONCEPTUALISE . . .

— When you have thoroughly explored the narrative, think about the function of storytelling. What role does storytelling play in our lives? For example, think about the centrality of stories to our childhood – fairy stories are used to teach us about the world around us (you might like to think about the lessons which *Little Red Riding Hood* is designed to teach, as opposed to *Jack and the Beanstalk*). Equally, think about how stories contribute to the construction of our belief systems. The New Testament in the Bible is, you could argue, a set of stories through which we learn – just as we did as children listening to fairy stories – how to behave, and what to expect from others.

INDIVIDUALISE . . .
— When you have had a chance to think about the importance of storytelling to our lives, focus your attention upon a
particular type of story: the myth. What is a myth, and how
does it vary from a story? How do myths originate? What do
we learn about a community through its myths?

RESEARCH AND COMPARE . . .
— Find out about any one or two of these figures from classical mythology.

● Cupid and Psyche
● Ariadne and Theseus
● Apollo and Marsyus
● Jove and Semele
● Prometheus

— Once you have learned the bare bones of the stories – by
looking them up in a book of Greek and Roman legends if
necessary – ask yourself what 'morals' you can draw from them.

LINK . . .
— When you have explored classical myths, turn your attention back to the text and think about what this myth is warning
Dora against. Think also about what this myth tells you about
the community. What do you learn about Imber? What rules
does the story establish? Also think about the nature of storytelling – how many storytellers, for example, do you encounter
in this novel? Whose stories do you hear, and how does the
identity of the narrator influence your understanding? You
might like to rewrite the myth Paul tells Dora from a different
character's perspective: Michael to Toby, Nick to Michael, Paul
to James. How does who is speaking and who is listening change
the story itself?

EXTEND . . .

— As you work your way through the novel, keep the idea of the myth at the back of your mind and watch out for episodes in which it resurfaces. How does Murdoch reinforce its strength, through the plot of the novel?

CHAPTER 4
(pp. 46–58)

Focus on: devices

INVESTIGATE . . .

In all kinds of narrative forms – whether plays, poems, television programmes or novels – writers and artists have relied upon structuring devices to move the action forward. A 'plot device' is a technique whereby the writer uses a particular situation or form of communication to give the reader or audience a large amount of information quickly without intruding upon the novel or play. Often, for example, in order to convey information to the reader, or audience, characters receive letters in which important information about the protagonists or the plot is conveyed quickly and easily to the audience.

— Try to come up with three examples of a plot device. You could look at *Hamlet* (c. 1603) and other Shakespeare plays. The opening scene of *Hamlet*, for instance, introduces the idea of the ghost of Hamlet's father and this is how we learn about his untimely death and the mystery surrounding it. Try to draw your samples from a wide range – take at least one of your examples from a novel.

CHOOSE . . .

— In this chapter Murdoch uses a plot device both to impart information to the reader, and to set up particular expectations

27

for the rest of the novel. What is this plot device? Work through it, focusing particularly on the details. What exactly are you told, and how does it move the action forward? What information is, very deliberately, withheld?

DELINEATE . . .

— When you have explored the plot device in this chapter, use your analysis to think about how authors manipulate readers through the structure of their works. You may want to return to this question at the end of the novel, thinking particularly about how beginnings and endings are constructed.

CHAPTER 5
(pp. 59–77)

Focus on: religion

RESEARCH AND CONSIDER . . .

— This chapter falls into two parts (pp. 59–73 and 73–7). The first part features Mrs Mark and Dora, the second follows Dora on her trip into town. Use the entire chapter to explore the religious values that the community adheres to, and consider the extent to which Dora disobeys, or *transgresses*, these values.

— What kind of community is Imber? Is it, for example, religious or secular? Is it Christian? Using the information you are given in the text, establish what 'Christian values' are. How are the values presented in this chapter particularly focused upon female 'goodness', and the idea of feminine religious virtue? How are the nuns established here, by Mrs Mark, as the epitome of female correctness under God, and how does Dora establish herself, through her actions in this chapter, as the *antithesis* of this position?

EXPLORE . . .
— What differences do you identify in the men's religious position? Do they oppose one another directly or indirectly? What religious values do the men espouse, in contrast, perhaps, to the women in this chapter?

COMPLICATE . . .
— Having considered some of the religious values advanced here you might like to think, in terms of the novel as a whole, about Imber's relationship with Eden, or Paradise – is the community, or the nunnery, set up as heaven on earth? Come back to this question as you work your way through the text, and pay particular attention to Toby and Catherine. Use the following questions as a springboard for your discussion:

- How many different versions of Eden are you presented with in this novel? (Remember to consider the silence of the women of the convent you are presented with compared with Dora and Catherine.)
- How does Satan, or the Serpent, occur in the novel?
- Who might represent Adam and Eve in this novel?
- How do the arguments over the bell work as a *paradigm* for the 'apple'? How is knowledge here seen as demystifying and alienating, paralleling Adam and Eve's expulsion from Paradise?

CHAPTER 6
(pp. 78–98)

Focus on: the theme of community

CONCEPTUALISE . . .
— As Michael wakes to the sound of the bell, this chapter

takes us back through the history of the community and, in the second half, we witness our first official 'meeting'. Select passages from this chapter and think about the extent to which Michael facilitates the creation of the community of Imber. What cracks are apparent in the community as this history is narrated? What attempts are made at the party meeting to re-cement the group?

EXTEND . . .

— Consider the idea of 'community'. How is a community formed? Think about yourself: what communities do you consider yourself to be a member of, and how do you identify yourself as part of those communities?

— While discussing the idea of a community, think about this passage and the idea of inclusion and exclusion. You have considered what you share with other members of the communities you have identified, but think also about how that automatically excludes some people from membership. How important is this exclusion in defining what makes up a community? You might like to discuss examples, such as asylum, and becoming part of a national community. If some communities seem straightforward, such as gender, then which community does a transsexual belong to?

CHAPTER 7
(pp. 99–118)

Focus on: plot

DETAIL . . .

— By this point in the novel you have been given a great deal of information about the history of Imber, but in Chapter 7 you are given a fresh insight into one of the novel's protagonists.

Work your way through this chapter and note down this information. What are you told here about the plot of *The Bell*, and more specifically, what are you told about Michael's history?

— Form a chronology, or time-line, of the events narrated here – write them out as a list in the order in which they actually occurred. (Note that this will not be the same as the order in which you, in reading the novel, find out about these events.) You may find this time-line a useful tool for analysis as you work your way through the novel.

CONSIDER . . .

— When you have created your time-line for the text, look at the amount of information you are given here. Are you surprised to find you are told so much about the protagonist at this point in the tale? How does this change your attitude to the novel? Think particularly about the opening sentences of the chapter: 'Michael had known Nick Fawley for a long time. Their acquaintance was a curious one, the details of which were not known to the other members of the Imber community' (p. 99).

— Does this plot detail make the story more mysterious? If so, why? Why does Murdoch emphasise that the rest of the community does not know what the reader is about to be told? Does this section increase your sympathy for Michael? Be specific about how the text manipulates our reaction to Michael and Nick in this chapter.

— Before moving on to work on the bulk of the novel, think about the nature of plot. What expectations, in terms of plot, has this chapter created for you as a reader? Think about how these plot details have affected your reading.

FORM AN OVERVIEW . . .

— Throughout your analysis of the text, the question of plot

in *The Bell* comes up again and again. You might like to devote a particular section of your notes to how the plot is constructed.
— Sketch out some issues affecting plot: for example, how many times are you told the same story? What changes occur in the plot? Which details are different in each telling? You will find these notes useful for focusing your attention, but also as a way of recording your changing attitudes to the novel. In this way you will be able to examine how your developing analysis differs from the interpretations you made at the start of your reading.

Focus on: romance

DISCUSS . . .
— Get together as a group and talk about the model of romance you encounter in this chapter. Is this the first love story of the narrative? Do you feel comfortable with it as a love story? If not, why not?
— In order to inform your discussion you might like to look at other homoerotic narratives and cultures. One example might be the civilisation of ancient Greece, where the young male was revered as the epitome of beauty, rather as young women are treated today. What kind of romance is sketched out here? Work closely through the chapter picking out examples of the two characters' feelings for one another. For example, do we ever get an account of Nick's feelings from Nick? How do you characterise their relationship – is it in fact a romance? Or is it, rather, a friendship, a 'crush', or a paternal closeness? To what extent do you perceive it to be a sexual relationship?

RELATE . . .
— You may want to compare and contrast this relationship with that of Paul and Dora's as narrated in the opening

chapter. How do the two relationships differ in development? Which appears to be less damaging initially? If you are reading this book with a friend, or in a group or class you are likely to disagree in your responses to these questions, so remember always to use textual evidence to support your different positions.

CHAPTER 8
(pp. 119–30)

Focus on: traps

DESCRIBE AND TRANSFORM . . .

— In this chapter we witness Peter trapping and releasing birds. Choose one of the characters witnessing this event and rewrite this episode from their perspective.

— When you have completed this task you might like to swap attempts with someone else who has done the same exercise. You will find that this highlights how differently the story is understood when seen through the eyes of another character. You might also find that your own understanding of events contrasts with – or even contradicts – someone else's understanding.

INTERROGATE . . .

— Through your rewriting and 'transforming' of this episode you will have become particularly aware of what occurs in this chapter. Use your own revision and manipulation of narrative voice to think about why Murdoch decides to give you this particular episode at this moment in the narrative. Why does Peter, a peripheral character, feature at this point in the text?

PONDER AND LET YOURSELF IMAGINE . . .

— Having thought about the construction of this chapter, extend your analysis to consider the metaphor of the 'trap' itself. Then ask yourself these questions:

- How many other traps are there in this story?
- Who escapes from them?
- Do different characters appear to be trapped, and who do you perceive to be acting in the role of 'trapper'?

— Return to this metaphor as you continue your analysis of the novel as a whole. When you have read to the end of the book, ask yourself how your idea of a trap shifts in the course of your reading and, especially, as you approach the end of the novel.

CHAPTER 9
(pp. 131–9)

Focus on: the theme of sin

CONSIDER . . .

'A belief in Original Sin should not lead us to probe the filth of our minds or regard ourselves as unique and interesting sinners. As sinners we are much the same and our sin is essentially something tedious' (pp. 131–2).

— From your reading of this novel how do you understand the phrase 'original sin'? What role does the idea of knowledge play in the fall from grace of Adam and Eve?

— In contemporary society we tend to prize knowledge and reward those that seek it. How is this at odds with the idea of Eve and the apple? Think about the understanding of knowledge in the Eden story, and how alien it is to us as a concept.

— Explore how 'original sin' extends from the fall of Adam and Eve through the characters at Imber. Concentrate upon the idea of division and dissension. How are relationships continually split through jealousy and desire here? Also look at the association of knowledge with trickery, suspicion and the failure to trust in God. How is the idea of knowledge associated here with what we might regard as 'negative' qualities?

HISTORICISE AND DEVELOP . . .
— The history of the notion of 'original sin' is long and complex but certain examples remain central in terms of its literary treatment. One important treatment of the concept is in John Milton's *Paradise Lost* (1667). Another is in Thomas More's *Utopia* (1516). If you have read – or would like to read – either of these works, then they would give you a useful background for the understanding of this idea in *The Bell*. How do these seminal writers understand the idea of 'original sin'? What is their version of knowledge? Do they regard it as the antithesis of faith? (You might think about how one could go about proving the existence of God empirically, in order to clarify your thoughts.)

REVISE . . .
— At this point you might like to return to questions raised in the 'Focus on: religion' exercises that we suggested for Chapter 5. In particular, revisit and revise your answer to the question of who represents Adam and Eve in this novel. How does your understanding of Michael affect your responses to these questions?

CHAPTER 10
(pp. 140–8)

Focus on: the bell

COUNT . . .

— Before beginning your analysis of this chapter, establish where, in terms of the novel's structure, this episode falls. How does its position alter your attitude to the chapter as a whole?

QUESTION AND ANALYSE . . .

— Consider this episode's relationship to the previous chapter. How does your understanding of the idea of 'original sin' and the notion of 'knowledge' change your attitude to Toby's curiosity?

CHAPTER 11
(pp. 149–58)

Focus on: language, structure and vocabulary

IDENTIFY . . .

— Work your way through this chapter and identify the phrases that set up the day trip as a 'special' event. How does the language and structure set it apart from other days at Imber? Focus on the events themselves and on how the unusual character of this day is established through context. In particular, how is the setting different? The characters are depicted in an unusual way here – consider how, without forgetting to include Nick in your analysis.

— What particular words and phrases are used to set this chapter apart from the rest of the novel?

CHOOSE, COMPARE AND CONTRAST . . .

— When you have conducted a close analysis of this chapter, you might want to compare and contrast its language and structure with other 'special' episodes in the novel. Select a chapter you consider to be particularly important and pick out the differences and similarities in style and language you have identified.

— How does this close work change your attitude to the story itself?

CHAPTER 12
(pp. 159–70)

Focus on: homosexuality

DEFINE . . .

— Establish your understanding of 'homosexuality'. What is its dictionary definition? What does the 'homo' part of the word mean and what is its linguistic root? What does its opposite – 'hetero' – mean, according to the dictionary definition? How does your understanding of 'homosexual' differ from that of 'gay' or 'lesbian'? Before extending your analysis, discuss contemporary society's interest in people's sexual preferences. Use the following questions to frame and locate your discussion:

- Has history always understood homosexuality in the same way?
- Do you consider contemporary society to be intolerant of homosexuality?
- What kind of abuses have homosexual communities been subject to – physical, verbal, social?
- To what extent is homosexuality treated as 'unnatural' or deviant?

- Why is homosexuality considered a ripe target for comedy? (List examples if you can.)
- What contrasting attitudes to homosexuality have been voiced by members of the Christian churches?

RELATE . . .

— When you have considered these questions turn your attention back to this chapter. Do you consider either or both of the men you encounter in this part of the book to be homosexual? If so, why – and how do their anxieties about social exclusion fit with your consideration of contemporary society's attitudes?

COMBINE . . .

— Using your close work with the chapter, along with the notes you made in your discussion in the first part of this section, answer the following questions:

- 'Contemporary attitudes to homosexuality are infinitely more tolerant than the responses that concern Michael and torment Nick.' Discuss.
- 'The language in which homosexuality is discussed in this chapter employs a totally different vocabulary to that used in contemporary society'. Do you agree?

CHAPTER 13
(pp. 171–80)

Focus on: boundaries

REFLECT AND ANALYSE . . .

— Think about the nature of crossing forbidden boundaries and the relationship of transgression to growing up. Come up with examples, either personal or fictional, where the idea of maturing is suggested by crossing boundaries. How far do you think adulthood is about being able to cross boundaries and thus assert our individuality?

— Thinking particularly about the importance of boundaries as we develop through adolescence, focus on the use of boundaries here. How does Toby come to question his boundaries after his encounter with Michael? How are they transgressed? Look particularly at the challenges the boys make in terms of boundaries. How are physical boundaries used here to mirror personal and moral ones?

REFOCUS . . .

— Using the ideas you have developed in the previous section, think particularly about how Toby reasserts his own boundaries in this chapter. How is this *epitomised* in his consideration of Dora?

ASSESS THE TERM . . .

— While you are thinking about boundaries, consider also how often experience and categories cross over boundaries and are neither one clear thing nor the other. The concept here is one of liminality – being on the threshold, or border of something. Look up the term in the Glossary – it is a useful word and worth looking out for in everything you read. Windows, doors, borders, fences, inside and outside, looking in, looking out, mirrors and definitions of self and identity are places and moments which might be described, or interpreted, as 'liminal', and by identifying such moments or scenes you should be able to assess crucial episodes and key moments in your reading.

CHAPTER 14
(pp. 181–91)

Focus on: town versus country

MAP . . .

— In this chapter Dora decides to flee to London. Use a map to trace Dora's journey around London. You may also want to search on the Internet for pictures of the places Dora mentions and the art she sees as we follow her around the National Gallery. Then consider the effects caused by these allusions to real places and real works of art.

DISTINGUISH . . .

— Think about what London is used to represent. How is the idea of the city set up in contrast to the countryside, or rural lifestyle, that Imber epitomises? Paying particular attention to the language, what phrases and clauses set London apart from Imber? You may also want to compare and contrast the 'urban' characters, such as Noel, with the country protagonists, such as Michael.

DEVELOP . . .

— What values are represented by the idea of the city in this novel? Does *The Bell*'s version of the country represent opposite values? You may want to draw up a table so that you can note these oppositions more clearly.

— At this point you could extend your analysis by looking at literature focusing upon these contrasts. Perhaps the most famous critical text is Raymond Williams's *The City and the Country* (1985), which explores ideas about the perceived opposition between urban and rural constructs.

CHAPTER 15
(pp. 192–9)

Focus on: the theme of knowledge

DETAIL AND CONTRAST . . .

— "'Well, look,' said Dora, "don't tell anyone. Let it be *our* secret now, will you?"' (p. 197). Using the character of Toby, consider this section's discussion of 'knowledge'. Compare Toby's choice to keep Dora's secret with his decision, at this point, to keep silent about his encounter with Michael.

— Paul is at both ends to the spectrum here, as he is the one both to discover and to receive information. Does he suggest that knowledge is a good thing? Is it useful? What does Murdoch suggest by putting him in both roles?

— Now think about what you take 'knowledge' to mean. Is it a positive notion? What do you associate it with? Is yours the same version of 'knowledge' as you are given by Toby?

COMPLICATE . . .

— Does Toby's knowledge empower him, or does it work to his detriment? Do you consider him to be in control of the knowledge he has?

EVALUATE AND REVISE . . .

— Look now at the end of the chapter when the characters agree to collude in their secret. How is knowledge represented here? (You may want to return to your consideration of the doctrine of original sin in the exercises on Chapter 9.) Is the imparting of knowledge a gift here, or a threat?

CHAPTER 16
(pp. 200–9)

Focus on: tension

EXAMINE . . .

— 'Peter Topglass sat in the third row, busy polishing his spectacles on a silk handkerchief . . . He was always nervous when Michael spoke' (p. 200). Try to define the different kinds of tension played out in this chapter. As well as the strain Michael feels in his relationship to Toby, in the quotation above it is Peter Topglass who is tense, or 'nervous'. Which other characters seem strained in their contact here? Don't simply focus on the main characters in the chapter but extend your focus to consider apparently peripheral relationships.

ASSESS . . .

— Use your analysis of the various tensions at play here to think about different kinds of tension and how they operate. Use the list below to stimulate your analysis – the parentheses suggest possible interpretations, but try and develop your own as well.

- Sexual
- Physical
- Environmental (for example, some people find that particular spaces – woods, bridges, big buildings – make them tense and uncomfortable)
- Emotional (grief, depression)
- Repressed feelings (anger, love)
- Intellectual (a difference of opinion, realising one has failed to understand)
- Social (excluding someone)
- Psychological (feeling excluded or isolated)

You may decide that more than two characters are linked by one strain, or tension, or that one character is subject to more than one form of tension. This is an important part of your analysis, so take care to explore these different dimensions as fully as possible.

RELATE TO THE WHOLE TEXT . . .
— In the light of your work on the tensions in this chapter, consider how tension works in this text as a whole. Do certain forms of tension dominate? Does Murdoch play upon tensions built up between the reader and the community just as she excludes and alienates characters? Do you, as a reader, feel in possession of the 'knowledge' that appears to elude the community at Imber?
— You may want to use the list above to interrogate the text as a whole, perhaps by picking chapters that you found particularly engrossing and thinking about how tension operates in them.

QUESTION . . .
— 'No one is ever relaxed or happy, the novel works to the extent that it draws the reader into this spider's web of tension.' Discuss.

CHAPTER 17
(pp. 210–22)

Focus on: mechanics and technicality

DISCOVER . . .
— In this chapter the reader is given a close account of the technical difficulties in carrying out the secret mission to drag the bell from the lake. Find answers to the following questions:
● When was this novel published?

- What three items that you now use on a daily basis were yet to be invented when this novel was published?
- Who was Prime Minister, which political party did they represent, and how long were they in power?
- What fashions is this year famous for?

CONTEXTUALISE . . .

— Use the information you have gleaned to start to construct your context for this novel. Think particularly about Murdoch's decision to be highly specific in some technical and mechanical details, while she chooses to sweep over the novel's political context.

— Consider in particular what kind of a context this chapter gives you. How does the information about the bell's movements give you a clearer map of Imber by repeating information about the community's layout, for example?

CHAPTER 18
(pp. 223–7)

Focus on: portents

FIND . . .

— 'Michael Meade was awakened by a strange hollow booming sound which seemed to come from the direction of the lake' (p. 223). This motif of the bell, and its signal of doom, runs throughout the novel. Look back over the text and select examples of this 'portent' that set up the reader to expect something terrible when the bell rings.

RESEARCH, COMPARE AND CONTRAST . . .

— When you have examined how the bell features as a 'portent' in this novel, try to come up with other literary examples of portents.

In particular, think about the imagery of 'bells' or 'the bell'. What are bells for? What does the ringing of a church bell, or a peal of bells signify? Might it mean more than one thing in different situations? What about bells on a clock tower, or a chime on a chimney piece? Some of your research might bring up works that are mentioned or alluded to in this novel. These might include Shakespeare's *Macbeth* (c. 1606). Look over the play and identify the place(s) where 'the bell' appears.

— Another literary reference is to a play called 'The Bells' (1871–72) that featured, famously, the same portent of 'the bells', spelling doom for another protagonist. Find out about that play. (A clue: it was a famous vehicle for the nineteenth-century actor Henry Irving.)

— In a third case, Victor Hugo's novel *The Hunchback of Notre Dame* (1833) – often mistakenly muddled up with the previous example – there are 'bells' which are rung by a deformed literary character. Find out about him.

— Choose either *Macbeth* or another victim of the power of 'the bells' to consider how portents figure in these examples.

— Who is portrayed as a 'witch' in this novel? You may also want to consider the treatment of the natural, the unnatural and the supernatural in *Macbeth* and its parallel in *The Bell*.

CHAPTER 19
(pp. 228–36)

Focus on: Communion and confession

DEFINE . . .
— Find out about the Christian sacrament of Communion and practice of confession. Who is allowed to take part – can anyone give or take Communion, go to or hear confession?

DISCUSS . . .

— Before turning your attention to the novel, talk over these religious practices. Have you or any of your friends taken part in religious ceremonies? What value do you place on these practices?

RELATE . . .

— When you have considered the nature of these devotions, turn your attention back to the novel. This chapter witnesses the first meeting between Michael and the Abbess, and we overhear a confession. Drawing on your own thoughts, and those expressed in your discussions, examine this conversation. Is the novel sympathetic to the idea of confessing your sins? Does Michael confess?

— Throughout your analysis you have looked closely at the role religion plays in this novel – how is this chapter's version of religion different from that portrayed in the novel as a whole? Are the Abbey and the House the same place, in terms of attitude, or is Murdoch careful to distinguish between them?

CHAPTER 20
(pp. 237–53)

Focus on: comedy

INTERPRET . . .

— This chapter could be described as 'farce'. Look over the chapter noting its comic and farcical elements. For example, which characters are made to look ridiculous? Traditional comedy often centres upon misunderstanding (from Shakespeare's *Much Ado about Nothing* (c. 1598) to the television programme *Friends*, jokes are often based upon two people making different assumptions), accidents of fate – like letters ending up in the wrong hands – and innuendo. Which of these elements are present in this scene?

— To what extent do you find this scene a change in tone and tension from the preceding chapters? How is this achieved, and which characters are introduced at this point specifically to provide some light relief?

INVESTIGATE AND REASSESS . . .
— Discover what the ancient Greek definition of comedy is. Does *The Bell* fit this definition? (You may want to come back to this question at the end of your analysis.)

RESEARCH AND COMPARE . . .
— In Shakespeare's tragic play *Macbeth* there is a famous comic scene where the Porter comes to open up the castle gate. If you know the play, look again at that scene and explore the ways in which comedy can relieve tension, only to set it up again.

CHAPTERS 21 AND 22
(pp. 254–60 and 261–8)

Focus on: the character of Nick

CHARACTERISE . . .
— These chapters are central to our understanding of Nick, as they are the only place where he narrates events himself. Hitherto you have been given an account of Nick mediated through Michael. Selecting particular words and phrases, construct a character analysis of Nick. Start off with his physical appearance and presence and work through to his psychological persona. Also, bear in mind the ways in which he is

characterised by his relationships, in particular with Catherine and Michael.

— How does silence work in our characterisation of Nick? What assumptions have you made about this character whom you meet directly only in the closing stages of the novel? Are they supported by these chapters?

— If you are reading this novel in a class or group, you may want to get together and compare and contrast your characterisations. Do others in your group have a very different version of Nick in their imagination?

ANALYSE . . .

— When you have completed your character analysis of Nick, think about how he works in terms of the plot. To what extent, given these two chapters, do you regard him as being in control at Imber? Does he intend Dora to overhear? Is it, in fact, a predetermined plan?

QUESTION . . .

— To what extent does Nick represent Satan in this novel?

CHAPTER 23
(pp. 269–80)

Focus on: denouement

DEBATE . . .

— Define *denouement* and when you have established your definition, consider the question: is this chapter the novel's *denouement*? If you are sharing your reading, get together in groups and, at the start of your discussion, vote on the question. Then appoint teams, one to argue for and one to argue against the motion. Remember to back up your argument with close textual analysis. Why should this chapter be regarded as the crux of the novel? Which other scene might contest for this title or definition?

CHAPTER 24
(pp. 281–7)

Focus on: the press

DETAIL . . .

— This chapter opens with a reference to the press. Read this section carefully, paying particular attention to the relationship of the press to the treatment of the events that have just been narrated. How does the text suggest the importance of representation through the role of the press here? Why are 'excerpts' from newspaper accounts included within the text?

TRANSFORM AND WRITE . . .

— Write your own newspaper article, setting out your version of events as they have been presented to you as a reader. What is your headline? What is your angle? Look over your 'report' and think about the selective nature of press reporting.

QUESTION . . .

— Interrogate the role of the media at this point in this novel. Is the text offering a critique of the press? Does Murdoch use the press to highlight particular versions of communities – the Abbey itself, or the lay community living in the house, for example? Think about the role of the press as you understand it. You may want to look at particularly famous media treatments of crimes involving O. J. Simpson,

Fred and Rosemary West, or Myra Hindley. Use the Internet to look at press treatments of these people. What shorthand terms are employed? How are these individuals represented? How are our own views and expectations being manipulated?

— Use these examinations to think about the role of the press in the novel, and how your reservations about the community are reflected in its press treatment. Are you, like the press, ready to see the community collapse at the close of the novel?

CHAPTER 25
(pp. 288–97)

Focus on: collapse and disintegration

DELINEATE . . .

— Consider the various forms of collapse you encounter as the novel draws to a close. Look first at the literal disintegration of Imber, and then extend your analysis to the relationships that are falling apart within that separation.

— When you have explored these elements of disintegration, focus on the collapse of the individuals themselves. Think about how the chapter's final gesture suggests a total crisis, in terms of sanity (Catherine), knowledge (Michael – who simultaneously knows too much about Nick and too little about Catherine) and faith (as explored by various characters in different ways).

REFLECT . . .

— Take some time to reflect upon the novel's treatment of religion in relation to collapse and disintegration. Does the formally religious disintegrate, or is it, in fact, visibly stronger at the close of the novel? Does the novel support a sustaining version of faith through the abbey? Is Eden sustained with sin cast out?

REVISE . . .
— In order to consider fully the issues raised here in terms of collapse and restoration you may want to look back over the novel, paying particular attention to Murdoch's treatment of the nuns. How are they characterised as a parallel to the House's residents? Use this revision to answer the following questions:

● '*The Bell* offers a redemptive version of faith and Christianity through the Abbey.' Discuss.
● 'In *The Bell* Murdoch creates a version of a Shakespearean tragedy. Human frailty becomes the "tragic flaw" that ensures the destruction of communities and individuals alike.' Discuss.

CHAPTER 26
(pp. 298–316)

Focus on: faith

DISCOVER, DETAIL AND DESCRIBE . . .
— In this final chapter Michael prepares for his changed life in the wake of Nick's suicide. Do you regard Nick's suicide as a sin or as a sacrifice? How does the Christian Church regard suicide?
— Detail the examples of faith you witness in this final chapter. Is religious belief still the link for those remaining at Imber?

EXAMINE . . .
Collate your results and look at the various examples of faith

you have discovered in this final chapter. Does the novel re-affirm Christian faith in its closing stages, or is its attitude more ambivalent?

RELATE . . .

— Think about how the novel's complex version of Christian faith works in relation to the critique of the religion you are given in this final chapter. You may also want to look back over the novel. Consider the claim that the text leaves you with an uncertainty that both criticises and supports belief and the sacrifices it demands.

Looking over the whole novel

QUESTIONS FOR DISCUSSION OR ESSAYS

1. Analyse the functions of the imagery of 'the bell'.

2. 'Nick, and his character, is the key to *The Bell*.' Do you agree?

3. 'The sublime is for Murdoch a central organising metaphor, discernible in her plotting, her ethics, her aesthetics, and her use of ordeals by love and water' (Peter J. Conradi). Discuss, in relation to *The Bell*.

4. In what ways do the patterns of ritual and romance structure *The Bell*?

5. How far would you describe *The Bell* as a criticism of solipsism and a proposal for community?

6. Is *The Bell* a comedy or a tragedy?

7. '*The Bell* is an illustration of Murdoch's own philosophical

resistance to pattern and shape. We have no destiny, we are simply here.' Discuss.

8. How far is the moment of transformative vision the central theme of *The Bell*?

Contexts, comparisons and complementary readings

These sections suggest contextual and comparative ways of reading these three novels by Murdoch. You can put your reading in a social, historical or literary context. You can make comparisons – again, social, literary or historical – with other texts or art works. Or you can choose complementary works (of whatever kind) – that is, art works, literary works, social reportage or facts which in some way illuminate the text by sidelights or interventions which you can make into a telling framework. Some of the suggested contexts are directly connected to the book, in that they will give you precise literary or social frames in which to situate the novel. In turn, these are either related to the period within which the novel is set, or to the time – now – when you are reading it. Some of these examples are designed to suggest books or other texts that may make useful sources for comparison (or for complementary purposes) when you are reading *The Bell*. Again, they may be related to literary or critical themes, or they may be relevant to social and cultural themes current 'then' or 'now'.

Focus on: the imagery of the bell

THINK ABOUT . . .

— How many phrases and expressions can you find that include the idea of the bell? Some of them might include: 'sound as a bell', 'time and the bell', 'bell, book and candle' or 'saved by the bell'. Find out where they come from. To what do they refer? When you've done this, consider what this suggests about the idea of 'the bell' and what it might represent.

FIND OUT . . .

— Think about bells in general. In particular, think about them in terms of cultural difference. How are bells used in Western culture and in Eastern culture? What are they used for? Which buildings have bells installed – whether large or small? What items might include a bell? What are they used to signal? Use this list to help you:

- Celebration
- Prayer
- Mourning
- Dinner
- Warning
- Calling people together
- Timetabling
- Announcing an arrival
- Indicating a presence

— Then consider how many different kinds of bells there are. Again, use this list to help you:

- Cowbell
- Church bells

- Dinner bell
- Doorbell
- Clock bell
- Cat bell
- Reindeer bells
- Town hall bells

— Ask yourself if there are particular occasions when bells are rung.

— Finally, ask yourself if there is any way in which all of these things might overlap. For instance: we are familiar with clock bells and with church bells, but might there be any sense in which church bells also – like the clock – mark the passage of time? In this case, think not just about daily time but about lifetimes.

COLLECT AND ASSESS . . .
— When you have collected as much on the topic of bells as you can, consider the imagery of the bell again in terms of the way that it is used in Murdoch's novel.

COMPARE AND ASSESS . . .
— Where do bells appear in literature? Think of as many examples as you can. These may include: *Macbeth*, *Cinderella*, Samuel Taylor Coleridge's poem 'Christabel', John Keats's 'The Eve of St Agnes', Goethe's 'The Roving Bell', Schiller's 'Song of the Bell', Dorothy L. Sayers's *The Nine Tailors*, Gray's 'Elegy in a Country Churchyard', Charles Dickens's *The Mystery of Edwin Drood* or *The Chimes* or *A Christmas Carol* or John Betjeman's autobiography in verse 'Summoned by Bells'.

Finally, consider this extract from John Donne's 'Devotions upon Emergent Occasions': 'Any man's death diminishes me, because I am involved in Mankind; And therefore never send to know for whom the bell tolls; it tolls for thee.'

Focus on: Iris Murdoch's ideas about the novel

RESEARCH . . .

— As well as being an eminent novelist and the author of some twenty-six works of fiction, Murdoch was an important philosopher and academic and a Fellow of St Anne's College, Oxford. Look at the list of all her novels and academic works in the Bibliography, and at the brief quotations from some of her philosophical works included in the Contexts section for *The Black Prince*.

— In 1961 Murdoch published an article entitled 'Against Dryness: A Polemical Essay'. If you can, obtain a copy of the essay. It argued that the novels of the twentieth century polarised into two groups: one group, which she characterised as 'crystalline', she described as being typically small, allegorical, self-contained, and designed to enshrine a network of themes (an example might be Virginia Woolf's *To the Lighthouse*). The other group, which she designated 'journalistic', consisted of large, rambling works, with many characters and containing both story and facts (an example might be Anthony Burgess's *Earthly Powers*). In both cases Murdoch saw these kinds of novels as essentially consolatory and ordered; comforting myths for both writer and reader. However, she proposed that the terms of her own work should be – in an imitation of life – not consoling, but involving chaos, chance, coincidence and contingency.

— By 1976 Murdoch said that she felt that the terms of her distinctions were too simplistic.

— After reading the essay, consider how far Murdoch succeeds in adopting her own arguments and methods in writing *The Bell*.

Focus on: Iris Murdoch

FIND OUT ABOUT . . .
Since her death Murdoch has become a heroine in the popular imagination. This is partly due to two recent biographies: *Iris Murdoch: A Life* (2001) by Peter J. Conradi, and *Iris: A Memoir of Iris Murdoch* (2000) by Murdoch's husband John Bayley. This last was particularly important for its account of Murdoch's final years when she suffered from Alzheimer's disease, and was subsequently made into the acclaimed film *Iris*.

— Read either of these biographies and watch the film. Given that so many of Murdoch's novels are about accident and contingency, as opposed to the transformative moment, you might like to consider how these elements are presented in the books or in the film. One important aspect to consider in thinking about the success of the film, is how odd it is that Murdoch had a successful, important and intellectual life, and yet the very things that made her achievement so unique – her philosophy and her writings – are missing here, where she is shown only at the beginning – when she hadn't done anything – and at the end – when she was debilitated and could do no more.

Focus on: Christian doctrine

— The reading guide contains exercises that focus on Christian doctrine about sin, confession and atonement (eg. Chapters 5, 9, 19 and 26). Refer to these exercises to form a framework of Christian teaching within which to situate the novel's concerns.

The Black Prince

IN CLOSE-UP

Reading guides for

THE BLACK PRINCE

BEFORE YOU BEGIN TO READ . . .

— Read the introduction and the section in this book entitled Interviews and Silences. From these you will be able to identify a number of themes that are discussed in *The Black Prince*. These themes might include:

- Eros or the Black Prince
- Envy
- The image of Hamlet
- Narrative method
- Writing and the writer
- Art
- Digression and delay
- Address, addresser, addressee

Other themes that may be useful to consider while reading the novel include:

- Light and dark
- Goodness

Reading activities: detailed analysis

Focus on: the title

RECALL, CONSIDER, IMAGINE AND ASSESS . . .

— What does the phrase 'the Black Prince' mean to you? There is a symbolic reference to the eldest son of John of Gaunt. If you aren't already aware of him then it might be worth your while doing some research into who he was and what he was like. Is there something romantic about the notion of a 'black prince'? Ask yourself what the juxtaposition of the colour black might imply when it is allied with the idea of 'princeliness'. Jot down as many ideas on this as you can, keep them to hand as you read the novel and add to your list as new meanings are revealed while you continue reading. You will be able to make many connections by the time you come to the end of the novel. Think also about the initials of 'the Black Prince'. That too will become relevant.

Focus on: the list of Contents and narrative shaping

ASSESS AND GUESS AT . . .

— Look at the list of Contents on p. 7. You will see two 'Forewords' and three kinds of 'Postscripts' listed. And, in the middle, 'Bradley Pearson's Story' is listed. What does this set up in terms of your expectations from the narrative which is to follow? Think about the functions of a 'foreword' and a 'postscript'. Also consider the ways in which Bradley's central 'Story' is effectively framed by these.

COMPARE . . .

— Try to think about other texts or novels that use this technique of 'framing' the central story. One example might be Mary Shelley's *Frankenstein* (1818) which is, in effect, a 'concentric' narrative where the creature's story is framed by Frankenstein's story, which itself is framed by Walton's letters home to his sister. Another example might be Emily Brontë's *Wuthering Heights* (1847) where the tale of Catherine and Heathcliff is told to Lockwood by Nelly Dean. Another might be Margaret Atwood's *The Blind Assassin* (2000) where the memories of the elderly Iris frame a realistic narrative in which she tells the story of her young life alongside two 'fictional' narratives – one inside the other – where two lovers meet clandestinely and tell each other stories about the imaginary planet Zyrcon.

— When you have come up with some examples of this kind, make a list of the expectations that such narrative techniques might set up. For instance: this may mean that your reactions are being manipulated not only by the novelist, but also by the characters in the story. Facts could be added in and told to you only after the events to which they related. On the other hand, the 'foreword' or framing story might give you information that you will look for as you read.

— Then ask yourself how often this happens in real life. Do you always know everything about a situation as it happens? Can you ever know what everyone involved in any given situation or event is feeling? Do you necessarily even know exactly how to characterise your own feelings and reactions? Might you find that sometimes they change, in prospect, in the event, in retrospect?

EDITOR'S FOREWORD
(pp. 9–10)

Focus on: storytelling

ASK YOURSELF . . .

— Consider the effect of this foreword or preface. How does it make you think about the story that will follow and what it might consist of? Who do you suppose is telling this story? Look at the ways in which 'Loxias' attempts to define himself on p. 10: as 'impresario', 'clown', 'harlequin', 'fool' or 'judge'. What does each of these titles suggest about the 'editorial' role?

THINK ABOUT THE NARRATIVE METHOD . . .

— 'P. A. Loxias, *Editor*' has some control over the narrative. He begins by saying 'I am in more than one way responsible for the work that follows' (p. 9). As we already know from the 'Contents' page this will consist of more than one narrative. Editors do sometimes appear in fictional narratives as one of the characters charged with collecting 'evidence' from other characters involved. Novels of this kind would include Wilkie Collins's *The Moonstone* (1868), and Bram Stoker's *Dracula* (1897). Bear this in mind as you read.

Focus on: art

NOTE AND CONTINUE NOTING . . .

— On p. 9 P. A. Loxias says 'Art is a doom'. As you read on you will see that epigrammatic statements of this kind about the character and function of 'art' appear throughout the novel. For instance, on pp. 11, 12, 13, 19, 50, 80, 124, 187, and so on. Whenever you come across one of these, note it down and see whether or not you have a consistent argument by the end.

AND COMPARE . . .

— Look up the Preface to Oscar Wilde's novel *The Picture of Dorian Gray* (1891). It also consists of epigrammatic and philosophical statements about the nature of 'art'. Compare Wilde's exploitation of this style with the methods employed here by Pearson (and Loxias and the other characters in the novel).

AND RESEARCH AND DECIDE . . .

— Loxias is one of the names of the god Apollo. He is often known as Pheobus Apollo. Find out who Apollo was in Greek mythology, and for what or whom he is the patron god. Also try to find out his other names. Why then might Bradley's editor be called 'P. A. Loxias'? What do you imagine that the 'P. A.' stands for?

BRADLEY PEARSON'S FOREWORD
(pp. 11–19)

Focus on: characterisation

CRITICALLY EVALUATE . . .

— When you have read this section, look again for the things that Bradley tells you about himself and make notes. Then close the book and brainstorm five key words which, in your view, would characterise what you know of Bradley Pearson. When you have done that, write a short description of him using all five of your key words. How does your own description fit with the description that Bradley gives you of himself on pages 23–24? Ask yourself how sympathetic you feel towards him.

ASSESS . . .

— 'As I now read this Foreword through I see how meagrely

it conveys me' (p. 19). Now that you too have read, and thought about, what this section tells you about Bradley, would you agree or disagree with this statement?

DESCRIBE . . .
— From the information you have here, write a short description of what Bradley looks like. He will give you his own version of his personal appearance later on.

Focus on: inverted commas

COMMENT ON . . .
— As you look over this section and as you read the rest of the book, note the ways in which Bradley uses inverted commas. Why do you suppose he does this? How does it affect the sense of the word or phrase conveyed to you? What might this technique tell you about his character?

Focus on: storytelling

NOTE . . .
— Bradley Pearson is supposed to be a novelist. Count up and note down all the 'writerly' references and allusions that you can find in this section. Include allusions to writing, texts, methods and literary quotations. What kind of a writer might you suppose Bradley to be?

LOOK FORWARD AND BACK . . .
— Note the number of times that Bradley refers to events to come and to his own ignorance of future events. How does this technique of anticipation help to carry you into the story? Remember to keep an eye on the number of times that he anticipates events in the course of his narrative.

Focus on: the theme of addresser and addressee

CONSIDER . . .

— Bradley seems to be writing with someone in mind – ask yourself who it might be. Is it Loxias, or his own self, or the reader? Remember that he seems to have some idea that something will be done with his testimony to make it public. How far, therefore, is this a genuine confession, and how far is it a public self-justification?

THE BLACK PRINCE
A CELEBRATION OF LOVE

PART ONE
SECTION 1 (pp. 21–31)

Focus on: beginnings

COUNT UP AND ASSESS . . .

— Note the number of times where Bradley's narrative discusses the need to shape a story with a beginning. Jot down as many examples as you can find. When you get to the end of the novel you will see why it might be that Bradley decides that this episode is a beginning.

Focus on: characterisation

LOOK BACK AT YOUR NOTES . . .

— On pp. 23–4 Bradley tells us what he looks like. How does this compare with the sketch you have already made of him in your imagination and as a result of reading his Foreword?

Focus on: the theme of delay and digression

NOTE . . .
— How many times does Bradley describe himself as 'delaying' in this section? As you read on, you might consider whether this need to delay and put off the moment of decision is a pathological characteristic in Bradley's make-up.

Focus on: the theme of envy

COLLECT AND ASSESS . . .
— Bradley makes several references to his relationship with Arnold Baffin in the course of this section. Consider how you would describe and weigh up Bradley's attitudes to Arnold in the light of the information you have been given so far. Choose from this list to help you: sycophantic, admiring, fearful, critical, despising, anxious, childlike, respectful, indifferent.

Focus on: names

CONSIDER THE SIGNIFICANCE . . .
— Names in novels are never accidental, though they may appear to be transparent. Rarely does a name come to us without accruing certain connotations and references. Look over this list of names and consider what things you might assume about a person who possessed such a name: Tarquin, Tracy, Saffron, Henry, Angelique, Bill.

AND IMAGINE . . .
— Let your mind wander over the names of the characters to whom we are being introduced here. Remembering the Shakespearean context of the allusions to *Hamlet*, if Marloe were spelt 'Marlowe' – rather than as it is – what might that suggest? Think about Christian's name. Is it an odd name? (There is a somewhat peculiar explanation for it later on.) And

what about 'Baffin'? Might it hint at a mix of 'baffled' and 'boffin'? Bradley, remember, does not want to be called 'Brad'.

Focus on: his flat

ANALYSE . . .
— Look at the description of Bradley's flat on p. 22. Think particularly about the 'womb' of the apartment and the 'erection' of the Post Office Tower. Then consider how Bradley's interest in things and careful description of specific objects contributes to your understanding of his character.

PART ONE
SECTION 2 (pp. 31–51)

Focus on: melodrama

RESEARCH AND CONSIDER . . .
— What do you understand by the term 'melodrama'? Look it up in the Glossary or in a dictionary of literary terms. Would you describe the scene in the Baffin household as 'melodramatic'? In what ways does it connect to the strict classical definition of the term? Use this list of forms to help with your ideas on placing the scene. Which ones might it most resemble? More than one term might apply: music hall, soap opera, sensation plays or novels, romance, tragedy, farce, slapstick.

Focus on: women, men and marriage

ASK YOURSELF . . .
— Think about the scenes where Bradley describes Rachel and her behaviour, and consider how flattering – or otherwise – his account of her is. What does this suggest about Bradley's attitudes not just to Rachel, but to women in general?

ALSO ASK YOURSELF . . .
— '"Rachel and I are very happily married," said Arnold' (p. 45). What do you think?

Focus on: death

LOOK OVER AND NOTE DOWN . . .
— Over the whole section there are a number of references to death and mortality – in particular look over pp. 38–9. Make a list of these references and think about the ways in which they influence your attitude to the scenes being played out here. Keep your notes – you will find them useful by the time you come to the end of the novel.

Focus on: styles of writing and writers

CONSIDER AND ASSESS . . .
— On pp. 49–51 Arnold and Bradley hold a conversation about writers and styles of writing. First, work out the ways in which this affects your ideas about the styles and achievements of each of these fictional writers. Then think about the propositions that each of the two men puts forward and consider whose side you are on. Third, if you look up the Contexts section for *The Black Prince* (pp. 104–106) you will see that there are a number of quotations from Murdoch's own philosophical works which deal with the subject of what art – and especially fiction – is for. Use these quotations to help you to ground your ideas about writing and style as played out in this discussion.

PART ONE
SECTION 3 (pp. 51–60)

Focus on: Julian

LIST AND ASSESS . . .

— This section introduces us to Julian and, in particular, to Bradley's conception of Julian at this moment in the story. Look carefully over the account of what she is doing and how Bradley misperceives what she is doing. Think about the number of 'mistakes' and readjustments that he has to make over the course of this encounter. Consider what this suggests about Bradley and his ability to see rightly, and consider also what the effect of this is on your attitudes and perceptions as the plot of the novel unfolds. Think particularly about the following issues: Julian as a young man then a young woman; Julian as stranger, then known; the 'flowers' that become torn pieces of paper; the 'Eastern' ritual that becomes something personal and specific.

RESEARCH . . .

— Julian is named after Julian of Norwich (p. 55). Find out about Julian of Norwich and keep the facts that you discover in mind as you read on.

TRANSFORM . . .

— Retell the story of this encounter from Julian's point of view. How does this exercise help you to focus on Bradley's character and your own assessment of him so far?

PART ONE
SECTION 4 (pp. 60–71)

Focus on: delay and digression

COUNT UP AND CRITICALLY EVALUATE . . .

— As you read this section consider how many times Bradley puts off doing something. Even the fact that he tells the beginning of his letter to Arnold, but then inserts a digression before he gives us the text of the letter, is relevant. Note down as many examples as you can. Ask yourself if you are finding this irritating. How far is this trait becoming a shaping characteristic, both in giving you an image of Bradley's personality and in patterning the storytelling method of the novel as a whole?

Focus on: letters and addresser and addressee

COMPARE AND CONTRAST . . .

— Bradley's narrative includes four interpolated letters that he writes and plans to send. Read these letters closely and consider how each one differs from the others in tone, in formality, in information given. Obviously they are written by the same person, but the fact that they are sent to different recipients means that they perform different functions. Remember that the novel as a whole is addressed to 'someone' who occasionally appears in Bradley's narrative as 'my dear' or his 'friend' – presumably P. A. Loxias. Compare and contrast the 'addressee' of the novel with the various 'addressees' of these letters.

Focus on: abortion

RESEARCH . . .

— On p. 70 we are given the story of Priscilla and her liaison with Roger, her pregnancy and abortion. For much of the twentieth century abortion was illegal in Britain, as it was in most

European countries. It was also expensive, risky and secret. Find out when abortion became legal in Britain and what arguments went into making it so. Find out also where in the world abortion is still illegal and why those governments keep that legislation on their statute books.

— Finally, ask yourself about your own attitudes to the subject. Abortion is still a contentious and difficult issue even in places where it is legitimate. Do some research on the subject by using Internet resources and consider the implications – for women, for children, for fathers.

PART ONE
SECTION 5 (pp. 71–82)

Focus on: women

LOOK BACK AND COMPARE . . .

— Priscilla arrives at Bradley's house in a distraught state. This is the second time we have been shown a middle-aged woman in such a condition. Look back at the scene with Rachel on pp. 34–42. Bradley admits to 'disgust' in his perception of Rachel. Consider how this second 'hysterical' scene also sets up an attitude of disgust in Bradley's view. Obviously – as he is telling the story – you can only know what he tells you. But how much of his contempt do you share?

Focus on: art and irony

RESEARCH AND EVALUATE . . .

— On pp. 80–2 Bradley offers a little digression from the plot in the form of a soliloquy on art and the function of irony in art. He describes irony as a 'dangerous and necessary tool' (p. 81). Make sure that you understand the term by looking it up in

the Glossary or in a dictionary of literary terms, then consider
the ways in which artists use irony to create a distance between
the facts of experience and our ordering and perception of
them.

— Ask yourself about the ways – even in everyday life – in
which we use irony to help to come to terms with facts and
situations that may be painful. Consider this scenario: you meet
a friend who has been bereaved, has broken a leg in a car accident, whose house has recently been broken into and who is
heavily in debt. Were you to say 'You've been having a bad
time lately' your friend might reply 'That's the understatement
of the year'. Instead of (justifiably) bursting into tears, your
friend is here using irony to cope.

— Consider Bradley's thoughts on this subject, evaluate them
and assess your own opinions on the matter.

PART ONE
SECTION 6 (pp. 82–91)

Focus on: structuring patterns

NOTE AND FIGURE OUT . . .
— Consider how each of the following incidents help to structure the story that Bradley is telling:

- Bradley notes the Post Office Tower glittering 'with newly
  minted detail' (p. 83).
- Hartbourne rings Bradley and suggests lunch (pp. 84–5).
- Priscilla goes on about her jewels and her mink and her
  vase (pp. 86–8).
- Christian rings and says 'Brad! I say, is that really you?'
  (p. 90)

— How many times have you already heard about the Post Office Tower, or about Priscilla's things, or about Hartbourne and his invitations, or about how Bradley does not like being called 'Brad'? The patterns are in Bradley's narrative, but we are also becoming familiar with them and aware of their holding more than just their surface meaning.

— As a reader whose critical function is to seek and create shapes in order to tell a story about this story – i.e. the novel as a whole – work out the metaphoric significance of each one of these incidents or references. Keep a note of when and where they recur, and keep reassessing their relevance in terms of the themes and patterns of the novel overall.

PART ONE
SECTION 7 (pp. 91–9)

Focus on: marriage

COMPARE . . .

— 'Marriage is a curious institution, as I have already remarked' (p. 91). Bradley has said several things about marriage in relation to Rachel and Arnold. Now he considers his own marriage to Christian. Close the book and try to remember the various things that Bradley has said so far. Jot them down. Then read this section and assess the ways in which Bradley's pontifications are the same, and the ways in which they are different.

RESEARCH AND COMPARE . . .

— If you have read Murdoch's *The Sea, The Sea* (1978) you will know that the protagonist in that novel also has a great deal to say about marriage. Compare and contrast Bradley's opinions with those expressed by Charles Arrowby in the later novel *The Sea, The Sea*.

Focus on: Christian

ANALYSE . . .
— Read Bradley's account of Christian's character and this first reunion with her. Then consider the information you have and come to your own assessment of her. How far do you agree with Bradley's account? And how is it that you are able to come to a differing point of view, given that all the information you are offered comes to you from his perspective?

PART ONE
SECTION 8 (pp. 99–110)

Focus on: the unreliable narrator

DISCRIMINATE . . .
Bradley says, 'The next thing was that I was in Bristol' (p. 99). Think about why this is an odd statement. Consider especially what Bradley's attitude to Priscilla's request that he go to Bristol for her has been up until now. How far can you trust anything that he tells you?
— As you read on, continue to assess – sceptically – his statements and attitudes. Here, focus particularly on his reaction to Roger and Marigold and their happiness. Notice also that on p. 103 Roger gives a different account of Priscilla's pregnancy, the abortion and their marriage. Who do you believe? And why?

Focus on: colour, light and dark

DISCERN AND ASSESS . . .
— As he gets drunk in Bristol, Bradley hallucinates and dreams. Look over this section on pp. 107–10 and note down all the references to colour and to light and dark. You may have noticed that Bradley often tells the reader that the sun is shining 'palely'

or 'coldly'. Keep an eye on these images as you continue. How do they contrast with, and connect to, the title of the novel?

Focus on: the theme of goodness

CONNECT . . .
— In his drunken state – or his retrospect on that state – Bradley addresses his 'dear friend and mentor' with a passage of philosophising about goodness and its role in the world (p. 108). How does this short section contribute to the theme of 'goodness' as it is discussed in the novel as a whole?

Focus on: fragments

ASK YOURSELF . . .
— The vase Bradley managed to take away is broken (p. 110). What significance do you read into this?

PART ONE
SECTION 9 (PP. 110–24)

Focus on: dialogue

TRANSFORM . . .
— There are several passages of straight dialogue in this section. Take one and rewrite it as a continuous piece of prose, but write from the point of view of some other participant in the scene than Bradley. How does this help you understand the implications of that scene?

Focus on: colour, light and dark

LOOK OUT FOR AND NOTE DOWN . . .
— The narrative offers a number of allusions to light and dark

and various colours in this section. Jot them down and work
out the ways in which this strand of imagery is being developed at this stage.

PART ONE
SECTION 10 (pp. 124–42)

Focus on: the theme of goodness

INTERPRET . . .
— 'The good feel being as a total dense mesh of tiny inter-
connections' (p. 125). How does the meditation on 'the good'
and 'goodness' in these pages contribute to the treatment of
the theme in the novel as a whole?

Focus on: electric-shock treatment

RESEARCH . . .
— On p. 126 Bradley considers the suggestion that Priscilla
should be given electric-shock treatment. This was a widely
used method of treating certain kinds of mental illness and
imbalance throughout the twentieth century, and is a practice
occasionally still used today. Find out about the treatment by
doing some research on the Internet or in the library. You might
like to read Hannah Green's *I Never Promised You a Rose Garden*
(1964), which includes an account of her treatment in a mental
hospital.

Focus on: structuring patterns

NOTE AND CRITICALLY EVALUATE . . .
— Several of the recurring structural devices appear in this
section: there is the letter from Rachel to Bradley; several references to the Post Office Tower – and to Bradley being like the

Tower, 'tall' and 'erect'; and Hartbourne calls. How does each, or any one, of these contribute to the patterning of the novel as a whole?

Focus on: Hamlet

RECALL AND RETAIN . . .

— On p. 137 Julian reminds Bradley that she wants him to help her with her work, in particular with preparing for an exam by discussing Shakespeare's *Hamlet* with her. He will do this in one extended scene, but in the meantime keep a note of any references to the play that you come across in the novel. If you have read the play, then look for any parallels that you can find in the characterisation or in the plot. If you haven't, then you might like to do so, as it will become a crucial parallel text, and provides a useful example of intertextuality.

Focus on: novels and novelists

NOTE AND REMEMBER . . .

— Murdoch likes occasionally to make jokes about herself and her own writing. Look at Julian's assessment of Arnold's novels on p. 137. Later on you will be given a list of Arnold's titles. See how many parallels you can make with Murdoch's own novels.

PART ONE
SECTION II (pp. 143–64)

Focus on: novelists

ASSESS . . .

— Bradley offers some thoughts on his 'explanation' or

'apologia' or 'treatise' over these pages. Read them carefully and assess how far and in what ways you trust him as the teller of his own story. Or maybe you don't, and if so, why not?

Focus on: light and dark

NOTE . . .
— Follow the light-and-dark imagery through this section. Add your observations to your notes on this subject so far.

Focus on: shops in novels

LOOK OVER . . .
— On p. 149 Priscilla and Bradley take up the theme of the shop where they grew up. This is not the first time this has been discussed. Look back over the novel to find other places where this was a topic of discussion or where Bradley told us about those early days.

RESEARCH AND COMPARE . . .
— When you have made your notes on the shop in this novel, look for shops in other novels. Examples might include: Charles Dickens's *The Old Curiosity Shop* (1841), Angela Carter's *The Magic Toyshop* (1967), Jeanette Winterson's *The PowerBook* (2000). How does the portrayal of the shop appear in each of these books? In what ways is it similar to that in *The Black Prince*, and in what ways is it different?

Focus on: childhood memories

REMEMBER AND WRITE UP . . .
— What is your own most evocative memory of childhood? Write an account of it. When you have done so, compare your account of your own memories with those that Priscilla and Francis tell. How does this help you to assess their characterisation in the novel?

Focus on: revelations

ASK YOURSELF . . .

— Francis reveals that he and Christian are Jewish. Bradley did not know this. What do you think that this tells you about Bradley?

Focus on: Hamlet

KEEP AWARE . . .

— Don't forget to be aware of the allusions and references to Shakespeare's *Hamlet* as you read on.

PART ONE
SECTION 12 (pp. 164–83)

Focus on: novels and novelists

QUESTION AND ASSESS . . .

— Bradley and Arnold have another conversation about novels, novelists and novel writing. Look back to the other episodes where they have had this kind of conversation and compare what is going on here with what happened there. In what ways are they covering the same ground, and in what ways are they developing their argument?

RESEARCH . . .

— Arnold tells Bradley that he is 'going to write a critical reassessment of [George] Meredith' (p. 173). Have you heard of this writer? Find out about him. (His dates are 1828–1909 and his best-known works are *The Ordeal of Richard Feverel,* (1859) *Modern Love,* (1862) *The Egoist* (1879) and *Diana of the Crossways* (1885)). Once you have the bare facts (even if you don't go on to read any of his works) ask yourself what this choice of subject tells you about Arnold.

IMAGINE, RESEARCH AND PLAY . . .

— Rachel says to Bradley 'the real drama is between you and him' (p. 179). Rachel – and other characters – have said similar things at other points. In a book published in 1985 and called *Between Men: English Literature and Male Homosocial Desire*, the critic Eve Kosofsky Sedgwick argued that this was a pattern typical in many texts of Western culture from Shakespeare's sonnets to François Truffaut's cult film *Jules et Jim*. That is, two men tussle with their differences and desires for each other, while the woman who seems to divide or unite them is actually irrelevant. Consider this in relation to *The Black Prince*. If you can, read Sedgwick's book. Then think of other texts that use this pattern.

Focus on: structuring patterns

FIND AND RELATE TO THE WHOLE . . .

— You will notice that there are several references – again – to the Post Office Tower in this section. Seek them out and consider the ways in which they contribute to the imagery of the novel, to the subtext of Bradley's passion and to the shaping of the story.

PART ONE
SECTION 13 (pp. 183–203)

Focus on: delay and digression

CONTEMPLATE . . .

— Consider the ways in which Bradley delays a) his own story-telling, and b) his departure from London for Patara. Work out how these two strategies – one literary, the other practical – parallel and reflect on each other.

Focus on: reference

RESEARCH . . .
— Look up 'Patara' in a dictionary of classical mythology. How does this help you in placing Bradley and the allusions that surround the idea of 'the Black Prince'?

Focus on: structure

ASSESS THE EFFECT . . .
— Bradley tells us that the 'first climax' of his story is coming (p. 183). What is the effect of this advice?

NOTE AND WEIGH UP . . .
— What structuring or patterning devices that you have already seen in the novel also recur here in this section?

Focus on: the theme of goodness

CONSIDER AND COMPARE . . .
— Bradley considers the nature of goodness and the role of the artist in documenting or creating goodness (p. 184). Consider this, keep a note of it and remember to look back at your notes when you come to the next section, where there will be more on the theme of 'goodness'.

Focus on: the theme of Hamlet

INTERPRET . . .
— Julian and Bradley's discussion about *Hamlet* comes effectively at the centre of the book (pp. 193–203). Why do you suppose this might be? If you know the play, what do you think of Bradley's analysis? Why do you suppose he gets so excited? How much of what he says applies to his own situation rather than to Hamlet's – or to Shakespeare's?

Looking over Part One

QUESTIONS FOR DISCUSSION OR ESSAYS

1.   'He has performed a supreme creative feat, a work endlessly reflecting upon itself, not discursively but in its very substance, a Chinese box of words as high as the tower of Babel, a meditation upon the bottomless trickery of consciousness and the redemptive role of words in the lives of those without identity, that is human beings' (p. 199). How far might this work as a description of *The Black Prince* itself?

2.   Consider the part played by the image of the Post Office Tower in the novel up to this point.

3.   Assess the importance of any ONE of these characters in the novel so far: Priscilla, Hartbourne, Julian, Oscar Belling, Bradley and Priscilla's mother.

4.   Describe the patterning structure of the novel so far.

5.   How would you characterise Bradley and Arnold's relationship, drawing only on your reading up to this point in the novel?

PART TWO
SECTION 1 (pp. 205–21)

Focus on: writers and readers

CRITICALLY EVALUATE . . .
— Bradley addresses his 'percipient reader' several times in this section. How far do you have the impression that he is speaking directly to you? How far do you have the impression that he may have some other reader – or readers – in mind?

What kind of relationship is set up here between the first-person writer of the text and the reader?

ASK YOURSELF . . .
— Do you trust Bradley?

Focus on: the theme of goodness

DEFINE . . .
— Bradley says 'I felt good. (I mean virtuous)' (p. 211). Throughout these pages Bradley meditates on types of 'goodness' and what that means to him in his present state. Consider the ways in which this section and Bradley's thoughts contribute to the discussion of the theme of goodness in the novel as a whole.

EXPLAIN . . .
— Why does Bradley have to add '(I mean virtuous)'? What is the effect of this pun, or qualification, or addition, in shaping your attitude to him?

Focus on: fragments

RELATE . . .
— On p. 215 Bradley buys Rachel a pile of presents in the stationer's shop. How does this connect to the shop he grew up in? How does it connect to Priscilla's lament for her lost treasures? Where else in the novel are 'things' vested with significance beyond their immediate importance?

Focus on: Roger and Marigold

LOOK BACK . . .
— Bradley sees Marigold and Roger (pp. 219–21). Look back at the episode with them that took place on p. 104–7. How

have Bradley's views changed about them? What do you make of this radical turnaround?

PART TWO
SECTION 2 (pp. 221–38)

Focus on: Bradley as narrator

IMAGINE AND TRANSFORM . . .
— On p. 225 Bradley mentions that he has – on an occasion he would like to forget – seen a woman in hysterics. Why do you suppose he makes this mysterious reference? Take five minutes and imagine what this scene may have been. Use a female character from the book if you like, or invent a new one. Then write up the scene from the point of view of Bradley. Try to convey his character as you have come to know it from your reading so far. How does this help you to discover how far you like, approve of, believe in or trust Bradley as narrator?

Focus on: time and philosophy

RELATE TO THE WHOLE . . .
'The division of one day from the next must be one of the most profound peculiarities of life on this planet. It is, on the whole, a merciful arrangement. We are not condemned to sustained flights of being, but are constantly refreshed by little holidays from ourselves. We are intermittent creatures, always falling to little ends and rising to little new beginnings. Our soon-tired consciousness is meted out in chapters, and that the world will look quite different tomorrow is, both for our comfort and our discomfort, usually true' (pp. 23–2). This is a key passage in the book and one that relates closely to

Murdoch's own philosophical sense of life as contingent and chancy.

— Read the paragraph carefully and consider how this connects to the methods and plot of the novel as a whole.

Focus on: lists and fragments

CONNECT . . .

— Bradley buys Julian some presents (p. 234). How does this list of objects connect to the other lists of objects that you have already noted?

Focus on: the Black Prince

COMMENT ON . . .

— On p. 235 Bradley says, 'I knew that the black Eros which had felled me was consubstantial with another and more secret god'. Take a few moments to think about what the Black Prince represents. How many 'Black Princes' have you met so far in the novel?

PART TWO
SECTION 3 (pp. 238–56)

Focus on: love and desire

ASK YOURSELF AND WRITE UP . . .

— Write up a short account of what it's like to be in love. How would you describe your own experience of love and desire? Tell the story of a particular encounter if you like. Your own experience may be useful as a point of comparison with the treatment of love and desire within this novel. In addition, your own experiences may enable you to understand and empathise with the characters.

RESEARCH AND COMPARE . . .

The poem by the 'Greek poetess' to which Bradley refers on p. 238, is by Sappho, who lived at the end of the seventh to the beginning of the sixth century BC, and is known as Fragment 31. Here is a short extract from the prose translation from the Loeb edition of Sappho and Alcaeus by D. A. Campbell.

> He seems as fortunate as the gods to me, the man who sits opposite you and listens nearby to your sweet voice and lovely laughter. Truly that sets my heart trembling in my breast. For when I look at you for a moment then it is no longer possible for me to speak; my tongue has snapped, at once a subtle fire has stolen beneath my flesh. I see nothing with my eyes, my ears hum, sweat pours from me, a trembling seizes me all over.

— How does this extract help you to assess the symptoms of desire in general and Bradley's in particular? Where else might you have heard such items of bodily reaction listed? Think about pop songs in particular: Shania Twain's 'Don't do that', Kylie Minogue's 'Fever' or 'Can't get you out of my head', Madonna's 'Do you like to . . . ?'. There are plenty of other examples that you will be able to find.

— How far does this suggest that these are the facts of what everyone feels in such a situation? Or how far is it the case that we simply *agree* that that is what everyone feels? Bear all of this in mind as you progress with these early stages of Bradley's passion for Julian.

Focus on: allusion and reference

SPOT AND NOTE DOWN . . .
— There are a number of quotations and allusions in this

section, particularly to Shakespeare's *Hamlet*, but also to other texts and to popular sayings. Try to spot as many as you can and consider why it is that they appear here and at this particular time.

Focus on: letters

INTERROGATE . . .

— Look at the letter on pp. 253–5. When you begin to read it you don't know who it is from, or what the situation – the 'mess' referred to, is. Did you guess? Or did you look over the page to see who it was from?

— Why is it important that Bradley should receive the letter just at this point? On p. 256 Bradley considers beginning a letter to Julian with the words 'My dear Julian, I have lately got myself into the most terrible mess'. Why would he begin this letter with these words?

— What does this juxtaposition suggest about Bradley and Arnold's relation to each other?

PART TWO
SECTION 4 (pp. 256–79)

Focus on: music

RESEARCH . . .

— The text here describes what it is like for Bradley to listen to music. It is a truism that music is a very hard thing to write about without resorting to imagery and metaphor. EITHER: Look up a literary description of music in some other novel or story. There is a famous description of a character listening to a Beethoven symphony in Chapter 5 of E. M. Forster's *Howards End* (1910). Or look at the advice and character of Klesmer, the singing teacher, in Chapters 5, 22 and 25 of George Eliot's *Daniel Deronda* (1876). When you have found a piece on music, compare it with Murdoch's description here. What does this suggest about the ways in which music (unheard, by definition, only imagined) can be used in the novel? OR: Find out about Richard Strauss's opera *Der Rosenkavalier* (1911). What happens in the story? Why is it relevant to *The Black Prince* that the character of Octavian – a boy – is a rôle written for, and always sung by, a woman? What is peculiar about the opening scene? What is the ceremony of the 'rose' and the significance of the 'rose-knight' or 'rose-bearer'? How might these elements connect to what is going on in the novel at this point? Listen to some of the music if you can. Do you feel that Bradley's account of the opening sections of the opera accords with your own experience of it?

Focus on: colour

COLLECT AND ASSESS . . .

— Much of the imagery in this section relates to colour. Note as many instances as you can and work out the way that the theme of colour is being played upon here. Remember that the title of the novel includes 'black'. What colour predominates here, and why do you think that might be?

Focus on: allusion and reference

RESEARCH AND CONSIDER . . .

— There are a great number of classical, literary and cultural references included in this section. Note them down and research the details to work out their relevance. These will include: Marsyus; Actaeon; St Paul's Church in Covent Garden (known as the 'actors' church' because so many are buried there); Ellen Terry; Marvell's poem 'To His Coy Mistress'; and 'older than the rocks' (p. 278), which alludes to Walter Pater's description of the Mona Lisa from *Studies in the History of the*

Renaissance (1873). There are many others which you may have spotted – all are relevant.

PART TWO
SECTION 5 (pp. 279–303)

Focus on: point of view

WHAT DO YOU THINK? . . .
— Read over the scenes that take place between Bradley, Rachel and Arnold. Whose side are you on, and why?

Focus on: time

ASSESS . . .
— There are a great number of references to time, timelessness and lack of time in this section. Note down the references when you come to them and assess their significance in relation to the discussions about time in the novel as a whole.

Focus on: symbols

CRITICALLY EVALUATE . . .
— Bradley gives the buffalo lady to Priscilla (p. 302). Think about the symbolic meaning of this item to each of these different characters: Bradley, Priscilla, Julian, Francis, Rachel. How does this help you to focus on the values important to each of these characters?

Looking over Part Two

QUESTIONS FOR DISCUSSION OR ESSAYS
1. 'This is art, but I was out there in life' (p. 205). Consider the balance of 'art' and 'life' as it is presented in Part Two.

2. What is Priscilla's role and function in Part Two?

3. How many times does Bradley change his mind in Part Two (about anything)?

4. List and assess the narrative patternings that shape Part Two.

5. How far does Julian's character develop in Part Two?

6. Describe the character of Bradley's relation with Arnold as it is played out in Part Two.

PART THREE
SECTION 1 (pp. 305–19)

Focus on: irony

ASSESS . . .
— This section covers the happiest moments of the novel. But how far are they undercut by irony, bathos, dislocation? Keep a careful eye on the tone of the narrative here.

Focus on: point of view

NOTE AND UNDERLINE . . .
— On pp. 307–9 Julian and Bradley argue about love. Underline the key words that each of them uses. Whose side are you on?

Focus on: the fall

RESEARCH AND COMPARE . . .
— On p. 309 Julian throws herself out of the car to prove the

truth of her love for Bradley. Think about the implications of the idea of 'the fall'. What is 'the Fall of Man'? What is a 'fallen woman'? How might these symbolic allusions help to focus and interpret Julian's action? What other famous falls can you think of? There is Louisa Musgrove's fall from the Cobb at Lyme Regis in Jane Austen's *Persuasion* (1818), or Senta's fall from the cliff in Richard Wagner's opera *The Flying Dutchman* (1843). Or you might find out about Mary Wollstonecraft's attempted suicide when she threw herself in the Thames, or the Greek poet Sappho's legendary suicide when she threw herself from the cliff of Leucadia. Try to make as many significant connections as you can to what happens to Julian. Don't be anxious about reading too much into it. That's what criticism is about.

Focus on: fragments

CONNECT AND ASSESS . . .

— On pp. 312–13 Julian and Bradley collect things; the sheep's skull, the stones, the driftwood. How do these fragments and meaningful objects connect to other 'meaningful' objects that we have met so far in the novel? Make yourself a list of as many such objects as you can. What does this tell you about invested meaning, as opposed to intrinsic value?

Focus on: love and desire

WEIGH UP . . .

— On p. 316 Bradley contemplates the specificity of desire. 'The absolute yearning of one human body for another particular one and its indifference to substitutes is one of life's major mysteries.' Think carefully about the range of his propositions here and assess your own attitudes in the light of your reading.

Focus on: Bradley as narrator

IMAGINE AND TRANSFORM . . .
— Look back at Part Two, section 2 (pp. 221–38), and the exercise about the woman in Bradley's past whom he had seen in hysterics. Here on p. 317 he again refers to some mysterious episode in his past. Why do you suppose he uses this repetition? Ask yourself again how far you trust him – given that he is telling this story.

PART THREE
SECTION 2 (pp. 319–42)

Focus on: Priscilla

JUDGE . . .
— What do you suppose Priscilla's role in the novel to be now? How far do you think that Bradley is to blame? Or anyone else?

Focus on: point of view

COMPARE AND CONTRAST . . .
— Think about the events of Priscilla's death, Bradley's actions on his return and Arnold's appearance at Patara. Focus on the point of view of the three main characters here: Bradley, Julian and Arnold. Jot down some notes on each of their reactions and attitudes to this sequence of events. Do you understand why Bradley did what he did? If yes, then do you see why Julian – and Arnold – may see it differently? What do you think about this chain of events?

Focus on: the Black Prince

ADD TO . . .

— Continue to note down allusions to the Black Prince, or to Hamlet, or to Eros. How is the theme extended and played out in this section?

PART THREE
SECTION 3 (pp. 343–75)

Focus on: love and death

SET UP OPPOSITIONS . . .

— Write down the places where 'love' appears in this section, either as a fact or as something discussed. Then write down the places where 'death' appears. How is the one set up in opposition to the other? Or are they connected in some way?

Focus on: patterns and narrative structures

LOOK BACK AND COMPARE . . .

— On p. 351 Bradley describes his despair and remarks, 'Odd that a demonic suffering should lie supine, while a glorified suffering lies prone.' Look back to pp. 203 and 206–7 where he first recognised his passion for Julian and compare and contrast the two episodes.

ASSESS THE LETTERS . . .

— Bradley recounts the texts of several letters here in order to 'advance the narrative' (p. 351). How does this compare with the ways in which the narrative has used letters hitherto?

CONSIDER . . .

— Hartbourne rings up (p. 354). He has appeared as a recurring structuring device many times now. What other example of such recurrences can you find in this section?

ANALYSE THE REFERENCES . . .
— Rachel suggests that Bradley is obsessed by storytelling of different kinds (p. 356). How does this group of allusions help to pattern the story here?

REMEMBER THE BEGINNING . . .
— Look at page 361 where Rachel says, 'I wanted to tidy things up. Now that everything has come out right in the end.' She refers back to the day when Arnold telephoned and asked Bradley to come over. Look back at that episode now (on pp. 21–51 of the novel), before you read the last section. You will see why when you have read the last section of Part Three.

Focus on: writers and writing

COMPARE AND CONTRAST . . .
— Look at the list of Arnold's titles on p. 364. Then turn to the beginning of your copy of this novel and read the list of Murdoch's titles. Can you find any similarities, and if so, what might that suggest?

Focus on: the Black Prince

CHECK FOR . . .
— Read over this section and note down any allusions that might connect to the theme of the Black Prince. Make a diagram showing how all the allusions and references you have collected may be connected and related to one another.

PART THREE
SECTION 4 (pp. 375–9)

Focus on: beginnings and endings

ASK YOURSELF . . .
— What are the similarities between what happens in these pages and what happened in the beginning? What are the differences? Why does it matter?

POSTSCRIPT BY BRADLEY PEARSON
(pp. 381–92)

Focus on: the unreliable narrator

ASSESS . . .
— Considering all the elements of Bradley's character you have worked on, do you believe his account of events here?

FOUR POSTSCRIPTS BY *DRAMATIS PERSONAE*
(pp. 393–411)

Focus on: point of view

DISCERN, COMPARE AND JUDGE . . .
— As you read each one of these statements, keep in mind the differing concerns of each character and their relative investments in the part of the story which most concerns them. Note the ways in which they talk about each other, including the way they each present themselves at the trial – consider details such as what they wear and what they say (and don't say). When characters contradict each other, make

a note of it. How many different 'Bradleys' are presented here, depending on the different perspectives of the speakers? Are you more persuaded by any one speaker than another? Why do you suppose that Julian and Rachel are estranged? What do you make of the changed surnames on two of the 'Postscripts'? What does that suggest about those two characters and what has happened to them since the events related in the main body of the story?

EDITOR'S POSTSCRIPT
(pp. 412–16)

Focus on: the editor

LIST AND COMPARE . . .
— In each of the four postscripts by Rachel, Christian, Francis and Julian, the characters make guesses at, or remarks about, P. A. Loxias's identity. Note them all down. Who do you think he is?

LOOK BACK . . .
— Reread Bradley's own postscript which is effectively addressed to, or written for, Loxias. How do Bradley's references in the postscript square with what Loxias has to say here in his own persona?

LOOK BACK AGAIN . . .
— Reread the first line of the novel. How does that statement read to you now in the light of your having read the whole novel?

Looking over the whole novel

QUESTIONS FOR DISCUSSION OR ESSAYS

1. 'I am in more than one way responsible for the work that follows' (p. 9). Consider the effect of this statement on your own expectations for the novel.

2. 'Only stories and magic really endure' (p. 13). Discuss, with relation to the novel as a whole.

3. Is Bradley Pearson the hero of *The Black Prince*?

4. 'The forms of bad art . . . are recognisable and familiar rat-runs of selfish daydream . . . [but good art] resists the easy pattern of fantasy . . . and often seems to us mysterious' (Murdoch). Consider this proposition in the light of your reading of *The Black Prince*.

5. Assess the importance of Shakespeare's *Hamlet* as a parallel text for Murdoch's *The Black Prince*.

6. Consider the importance of quotations and allusions to the patterning and structure of *The Black Prince*.

7. '*The Black Prince* is a long polished hymn to the reader's pleasure in unmasking and appreciating the unreliable narrator.' Discuss.

8. 'Far from being a novel of accident and contingency, *The Black Prince* is highly structured.' Do you agree? Explain your answer with close reference to the text.

9. What is the function of Rachel's role in the unfolding of the story of *The Black Prince*?

10. Assess Bradley's statement: 'This little book is important to me and I have written it as simply and as truthfully as I can' (p. 390).

11. Explain the literary purposes of the six postscripts.

12. 'Art is to do with joy and play and the absurd' (p. 414). How far is this statement borne out by your reading of *The Black Prince*?

Contexts, comparisons and complementary readings

These sections suggest contextual and comparative ways of reading these three novels by Murdoch. You can put your reading in a social, historical or literary context. You can make comparisons – again, social, literary or historical – with other texts or art works. Or you can choose complementary works (of whatever kind) – that is, art works, literary works, social reportage or facts which in some way illuminate the text by sidelights or interventions which you can make into a telling framework. Some of the suggested contexts are directly connected to the book, in that they will give you precise literary or social frames in which to situate the novel. In turn, these are either related to the period within which the novel is set, or to the time – now – when you are reading it. Some of these examples are designed to suggest books or other texts that may make useful sources for comparison (or for complementary purposes) when you are reading *The Black Prince*. Again, they may be related to literary or critical themes, or they may be relevant to social and cultural themes current 'then' or 'now'.

Focus on: philosophy

COMPARE AND ASSESS . . .

On p. 13 Bradley Pearson says, 'I have also emitted a small book of "texts" or "studies". I would not exactly call it a work of philosophy . . . Time has not been given me in which to become a philosopher, and this I but in part regret.' Murdoch herself was an eminent philosopher and academic, as well as a novelist. She was a Fellow of St Anne's College, Oxford, from 1948. Her academic books included *Sartre: Romantic Rationalist* (1953); *The Sovereignty of Good* (1970); *The Fire and the Sun* (1977); *Metaphysics as a Guide to Morals* (1992); *Acastos: Two Platonic Dialogues* (1986); and *Existentialists and Mystics* (1997).

— The following paragraphs are short quotations from various publications of her philosophical works. Read them over and consider the ways in which the concerns referred to here in Murdoch's philosophical works may overlap with the themes of her fiction.

> [Love represents] . . . the perception of individuals. Love is the extremely difficult realisation that something other than oneself is real. Love, and so art and morals, is the discovery of reality. What stuns us into the realisation of our super sensible destiny is not, as Kant imagined, the formlessness of nature, but rather its unutterable particularity; and the most particular and individual of all things is the mind of man.

From '*The Sublime and the Good*' (1959)

> Art naively or wilfully accepts appearances instead of questioning them. Similarly a writer who portrays a

doctor does not possess a doctor's skill, but simply imitates.

From *The Fire and the Sun: Why Plato Banished the Artists* (1977)

I can see no evidence to suggest that human life is not something self-contained. There are properly many patterns and purposes within life, but there is no general and as it were externally guaranteed pattern or purpose of the kind for which philosophers and theologians used to search. We are what we seem to be, transient mortal creatures subject to change . . . Our destiny can be examined, but it cannot be justified or totally explained. We are simply here.

The psyche is a historically determined individual relentlessly looking after itself. In some ways it resembles a machine; in order to operate it needs sources of energy, and it is predisposed to certain patterns of activity. The area of its vaunted freedom of choice is not usually very great. One of its main pastimes is daydreaming. It is reluctant to face unpleasant realities. Its consciousness is not normally a transparent glass through which it views the world, but a cloud of more or less fantastic reverie designed to protect the psyche from pain. It constantly seeks consolation, either through imagined inflation of self or through fictions of a theological nature. Even its loving is more often than not an assertion of self.

Almost all art is a form of fantasy-consolation and few artists achieve the vision of the real. The talent of the artist can be readily, and is naturally, employed to produce a picture whose purpose is the

consolation and aggrandisement of the author and
the projection of his personal obsessions and wishes.
To silence and expel self, to contemplate and
delineate nature with a clear eye, is not easy and
demands a moral discipline.

Of course great artists are 'personalities' and have
special styles; even Shakespeare occasionally, though
very occasionally, reveals a personal obsession. But
the greatest art is 'impersonal' because it shows us
the world, our world and not another one, with a
clarity which startles and delights us simply because
we are not used to looking at the real world at all.
Of course, artists too are pattern-makers. The claims
of form and the question of 'how much form' to
elicit constitutes one of the chief problems of art.
But it is when form is used to isolate, to explore, to
display something which is true that we are most
highly moved and enlightened.

From *The Sovereignty of Good* (1970)

Focus on: Hamlet

RESEARCH AND COMPARE . . .

— As a very famous text which has entered the language and
the popular imagination, *Hamlet* has been reworked and revised
many times. If you can't think of any examples of quotes from
Hamlet, consult a dictionary of quotations and see how many
famous phrases – that have now become clichés or truisms –
have entered our everyday speech. These might include 'slings
and arrows', 'The play's the thing', 'Alas, poor Yorick' and 'Get
thee to a nunnery', but there are many more. Once you have

your list, consider how many of these actually appear in *The Black Prince*.

RESEARCH AGAIN . . .

— How many works of literature can you think of that rework or revise or refer to *Hamlet*? Two well-known examples might be T. S. Eliot's poem 'The Love Song of J. Alfred Prufrock' (1917) or Tom Stoppard's play *Rosencrantz and Guildenstern Are Dead* (1967). Read either of these works – or any others that you can come up with – and compare the ways in which those writers use Shakespeare's play with the way in which Murdoch uses it in *The Black Prince*.

Focus on: fiction, popular, literary and esoteric

CONSIDER . . .

— *The Black Prince* is a novel about novelists. Consider the kinds of fiction currently available in the marketplace. Make a list. It might include: chick-lit, literary fiction, romance, thrillers, detective stories, psychological thrillers, murder mystery, lad-lit, faction. You will be able to think of others.

— How far do the principles that define 'kinds' of fiction lie behind the tussle between Bradley and Arnold? You might like to look particularly at the terms of Julian's definition of Arnold's kind of writing on p. 137. You might also like to refer to the list of Arnold's titles on p. 364.

— What kind of fiction does Murdoch herself write? Is it possible that she is making a self-referential joke?

Focus on: the late 1960s and the early 1970s

CONTEXTUALISE . . .

— *The Black Prince* was published in 1973. What hints are there in the opening section of the narrative about when it is set? The reference to the Post Office Tower will help you to place the time period. Is the novel set at the time of its publication, or slightly earlier? Use the Internet and any other resources available to you (there might be a copy in your library of the *Chronology of the Twentieth Century*, for instance) to discover what late 1960s and early 1970s London looked and felt like. Which musicians and actors characterise the period? What were the most popular films and television series? How did people dress in the period? What major political events took place? Which important novels were published at this time? Who were the sixties and early seventies icons? The following list suggests some starting points:

- *Don't Look Now*
- *Bazaar*
- *Love Story*
- The Beatles
- Harold Wilson
- Flower power
- The contraceptive pill
- The 1963 nuclear Test-Ban Treaty
- The Vietnam War
- *The Avengers*
- Motown
- Flares
- Laura Ashley

— You might also refer to *Sixties London*, photographs by Dorothy Bohm (1996), or to *Ready, Steady, Go! The Smashing Rise and Giddy Fall of Swinging London* (2002).

Focus on: the unreliable narrator

SEARCH AND COMPARE . . .

— Bradley may be an unsympathetic narrator and at times he is certainly unreliable – for instance, when he 'decodes' Julian's letter on pp. 369–72. In the end you have to decide whether or not he is 'reliable' and whether or not you can trust him. Find other 'unreliable' narrators in fiction: these might include the storyteller in Henry James's 'The Liar' or *The Aspern Papers*, (1888), the first-person narrator of Martin Amis's *Success* (1978) or of J. D. Salinger's *The Catcher in the Rye*. (1951)

— Compare any of these narrators with Bradley Pearson.

Focus on: Eros

FIND OUT . . .

— Research the legends about the ancient Greek god Eros. What are his special characteristics and over what does he rule? How does an understanding of that allusion help you to read *The Black Prince*?

The Sea, The Sea

IN CLOSE-UP

Reading guides for

THE SEA, THE SEA

BEFORE YOU BEGIN TO READ . . . .
— Read the introduction and the section in this book entitled Interviews and Silences. From these you will be able to identify a number of themes that are discussed in *The Sea, The Sea*. These themes might include:

● Theatre and magic
● Retrospect, autobiography, memoir
● Narrative patterning
● First love
● Chance
● Digression and delay
● Address, addresser, addressee

Other themes that may be useful to consider while reading the novel include:

● Enlightenment
● Goodness
● The Gothic
● The persecuted maiden

- The artist and the soldier
- The secret room

Reading activities: detailed analysis

Focus on: the title

RECALL, CONSIDER, IMAGINE AND ASSESS . . .

— What does the title of this novel suggest to you? Jot down your ideas, no matter how absurd or far-fetched. Also ask yourself: why the repetition in the title? Could this novel have been called simply *The Sea*, and in what ways might you have felt differently about it if it were?

— When you have finished the book you might also like to look at the Contexts section where there are some suggestions for possible allusions in the title.

Focus on: the Contents

CONTEMPLATE . . .

— There are three elements listed on the Contents page, 'Prehistory', 'History' and 'Postscript: Life Goes On'. What does this suggest to you about what you are about to read? Is there any way in which you can imagine this list of Contents linked to the title of the novel?

PART I, PREHISTORY
SECTION 1 (pp. 1–16)

Focus on: beginnings

CONSIDER . . .

— What do you expect from the beginning of a novel? In what ways does this opening match your expectations? In what ways might it subvert them? Then ask yourself what it is in this opening that is making you go on reading and how you are being encouraged to continue. Work out whether the main focus is character, plot, setting or style. Consider also the effect of the early introduction of 'something' happening that 'was so extraordinary and so horrible that I cannot bring myself to describe it even now after an interval of time'. Remember this. You will need to come back to it later.

COMPARE . . .

— Look at some openings to other novels. You could try, for instance, Jane Austen's *Pride and Prejudice*, Charlotte Brontë's *Jane Eyre*, Ian McEwan's *Enduring Love*, Jeanette Winterson's *Oranges Are Not the Only Fruit*, Laurence Sterne's *Tristram Shandy* or George Eliot's *Adam Bede*. Try to work out what main things are drawing you in in each case, and compare the other methods with Murdoch's.

Focus on: description

LOOK OVER . . .

— Look at each of the paragraphs in this section. Many of them are concerned with description of one kind or another: of the land and seascape; of the kind of narrative that Charles Arrowby plans; of Charles himself; of his house; of the pleasures and pains of swimming in the sea. Work out the different purposes of each of these different elements. Make a note of how many times each different subject described reappears. Then ask yourself what kind of pictures you have in your mind by the time you come to the end of this sixteen-page section.

Focus on: food

NOTE AND BEAR IN MIND . . .
— On p. 7 Charles tells us in detail what he had for lunch. Keep this in mind. You will hear a great deal about his meals as the novel progresses. The menu itself is followed by a lengthy account of Charles's attitude to and ideas about cooking and eating. Consider these and work out what this little riff tells you about Charles's character.

ASSESS THE PATTERN . . .
— You will, as mentioned, hear about many of Charles's meals. Consider them as a pattern. As you come across each one, think about it in relation to the others. How does this help to structure and shape the novel? If you have read Murdoch's *The Black Prince* you will know that Bradley's delays and digressions and pauses are one of the things that gives that novel a shape. Compare that strategy with this similar method in *The Sea, The Sea*.

Focus on: characters

NOTE THE EFFECT . . .
— On p. 3 Charles lists the names of a group of his friends: Wilfred, Sidney, Peregrine, Fritzie, Clement. On p. 15 he does this again, giving surnames for some that he has already mentioned and adding others: Al, Marcus, Gilbert. Ask yourself what expectations this sets up for you. When you have got to the end of the novel ask yourself whether or not your initial expectations have been fulfilled.

PART I
SECTION 2 (pp. 16–39)

Focus on: storytelling

ASSESS . . .
— Consider the effect of these statements:

- 'I seem to be constantly putting off the moment when I begin to give a formal account of myself' (p. 17).
- 'It has the expectant air of a stage set' (p. 17).
- 'I can describe this in no other way' (p. 19).
- 'I was utterly horrified in the kitchen this morning to see . . .' (p. 24).

— Think about each one. Then work out what each of them individually tells you about Charles, his character, his attitudes, his expertise, his style of speaking (or writing). Then think about them all together. How do these sentences – just on their own – advance the telling of the story?

Focus on: the horrible thing

LOOK BACK AND BEAR IN MIND . . .
— On pp. 18–22 Charles tells us about 'the horrible thing' that he had mentioned on the first page of his narrative. How horrible do you think this was? What do you suppose he saw? Try to identify what it might mean literally, practically, metaphorically and psychologically.

Focus on: Shakespeare

MAKE CONNECTIONS TO THE LIFE . . .
— We know now that Charles was an eminent – he says he was, anyway – director in the theatre. Then we are told on

p. 27 that he was born at Stratford-upon-Avon. Find out whatever you can about Shakespeare's own life by looking him up in a companion to English literature. In what ways might the terms of Charles's character, career and experience be compared with Shakespeare's? Think particularly about their backgrounds, about their names, and about what happened at the end of their careers. Bear all this in mind, as you will want to come back to it later.

MAKE CONNECTIONS TO THE PLAYS . . .
— On p. 29 Charles says, 'I fled to the trickery and magic of art. I craved glitter, movement, acrobatics, noise. I became an expert on flying machines . . .' Shakespeare's last play – or what is generally thought to be his last play – was *The Tempest*. The chief character, Prospero, is a mage or magician and rules over the spirits of the island he inhabits. At the end of the play he 'abjures' magic and goes back to his kingdom in Milan. Read *The Tempest* and consider the ways in which Murdoch may be using Shakespeare's play as a subtext, or intertext, for *The Sea, The Sea*.

Focus on: lunch

KEEP UP WITH YOUR NOTES . . .
— Notice the ways in which lunch – and Charles's other meals and shopping – is still providing a structuring pattern. Keep making your notes on this as they will be helpful to look at later on.

Focus on: storytelling

THINK ABOUT . . .
— On p. 39 Charles begins a section of his memoir, or diary, or whatever it is, by saying 'Something rather odd and distressing has just occurred.' Does this remind you of any

other passage in Charles's story? What is the effect on you – the reader – of these little shocks and horrors?

PART I
SECTION 3 (pp. 40–66)

Focus on: the enclosed space and the outside world

COMPARE AND CONTRAST . . .

— On p. 40, and again on p. 54, Charles ventures into the outside world from the enclosed space of his house (and tower). Look at these passages of dialogue and consider a) the ways in which they contrast with and counterpoint Charles's own narrative, and b) the way in which they suggest that Charles's story – and his enclosed world – is slightly askew.

Focus on: Lizzie

REFLECT ON . . .

— Lizzie is introduced substantially in this section. Note that the two roles that Charles mentions she played exceptionally well – and that he associates with her – are Ariel in Shakespeare's *The Tempest* and Cherubino in Mozart's *The Marriage of Figaro*. Look up these two roles. In what ways are they similar? Remember that Ariel is sexless and that the part of Cherubino portrays a young man who is always played by a woman. How does this contribute to your image of Lizzie?

Focus on: Hartley

ASSESS . . .

— Hartley, Charles's first love, is introduced for the first time on p. 52. How convinced are you by this picture of an ideal love?

Focus on: James

ASK YOURSELF . . .

— James, Charles's cousin, has already been mentioned. How important do you think he will be as the novel unfolds? Keep a note of your thoughts, as they may be useful later on.

PART I
SECTION 4 (pp. 66–89)

Focus on: the sea

NOTE . . .

— On p. 66 Charles reports a conversation in the pub about swimming in the sea and its dangers. Remember this. You will want to refer to it later on.

Focus on: writing

COLLECT AND KEEP NOTING . . .

— What do you think of Charles as a writer? You will notice that he solipsistically looks over his own work and comments on it with a critical eye. How does this make you feel about him as a narrator? Would you consider him an 'unreliable' narrator?

Focus on: Peregrine and Rosina

FIND OUT . . .

— Find out what the name 'Peregrine' means. Where are there any famous 'Peregrines' in literature? There is a famous Rosina (in music) – try to find out where. How does this kind of teasing out of allusions help you to define and focus on the literary creation of these characters?

Focus on: Hartley

CONSIDER AND COMPARE . . .
— Read over the passages that describe Charles's youthful relation with Hartley. How convinced are you by this? How does
Charles's story compare with other famous accounts of youthful
first love? Useful sources to consider might include:

- Shakespeare's *Romeo and Juliet*
- Emily Brontë's *Wuthering Heights*
- John Clare's poem 'First Love'
- Jeanette Winterson's *Oranges Are Not the Only Fruit*
- Charles Dickens's *Great Expectations*
- Elizabeth Gaskell's *Cousin Phillis*

Looking over Part I

QUESTIONS FOR DISCUSSION OR ESSAYS
1. Assess the significance of the imagery associated with the
sea in Part I.

2. How would you describe Charles's character from your
reading of the novel so far?

3. What is the function of 'the horrible thing' that is
mentioned on p. 1?

4. Is this a memoir, a diary, an autobiography, or another kind
of literary form?

5. Do you consider Charles Arrowby to be a 'reliable' narrator?

PART II, HISTORY, ONE
(pp. 91–110)

Focus on: past and present

INTERPRET . . .

— Gilbert says to Charles that he and Lizzie have 'sort of repossessed the past together and redeemed it' (p. 93). Charles's reaction to this is less than encouraging. Ask yourself these questions: How far might this be an exact description of Charles's enterprise? How far could this be an account of one of the major themes of the book as a whole?

Focus on: narrative and storytelling

NOTICE AND ASSESS . . .

● 'It is now two hours later and I am sitting in the little red room' (p. 99).

● 'Shortly after this something very disconcerting happened, and then . . . But first . . .' (p. 100).

— Consider these two opening sentences. How do they fit with Charles's narrative style? In what ways is this typical of his method? Keep noticing other examples.

Focus on: magic

MAKE CONNECTIONS . . .

Rosina says, 'Those women loved you for your power, your magic, yes, you have been a sorcerer. And now it's over.' (p. 108). If you look over this chapter, you will see that there have been a number of references to magic and the supernatural. Find as many as you can. Then ask yourself how this relates to the themes of the book as a whole, and to the many allusions to *The Tempest*.

Focus on: Hartley

HOW DID YOU REACT? . . .

— On p. 110 Charles recognises Hartley. What do you think of this moment and his reaction?

PART II, HISTORY TWO
(pp. 111–52)

Focus on: place and distance

DECIDE ON THE EFFECT . . .

— Charles tells us at the beginning of the chapter (p. 111) that he is now writing in London. What does this suggest about his perspective on the events that he relates? How do you feel about the honesty – or otherwise – of his narrative at this point in the novel?

Focus on: emotion

ASK YOURSELF . . .

— 'It occurred to me later that I never for a second doubted that her emotion was as strong as my own; although this could well have been otherwise' (p. 115). What do you think? Bear this remark in mind as you read on.

Focus on: Nibletts

ANALYSE . . .

— Read over the description of Nibletts and of Charles's visit there. This is the second house described in the novel. How does it compare with Shruff End? What is the tone of this description? Consider the social and class implications of this visit. Consider also the kinds of language and phrases used by

Ben and Mary. What do they suggest about either or both of them?

Focus on: myth

RESEARCH . . .
— 'She had, I remembered, walked behind me, not with me. How odd it must have looked though, with me as a crazed Orpheus and her as a dazed Eurydice' (p. 128). Look up the story of this Greek legend. When you have, consider why Charles uses it as a parallel for this scene with Hartley and think about the scene from his point of view.
— Then switch to Hartley's point of view. If he had said in the first person, 'It seems to me that I am Orpheus' etc., how do you think she would have reacted?
— Finally, ask yourself whether or not you think the analogy is appropriate.

Focus on: the sea monster

WHY? . . .
— Charles tells us that he was looking for the sea monster (p. 130). Why here, and why now?

Focus on: lunch

INTERPRET . . .
— Charles says, 'I had no heart to cook lunch' (p. 139). What does this tell you? Are you still noting the food? Jot down any changes in this pattern.

Focus on: history and prehistory

DEFINE . . .
— These are the titles Charles gives to the sections of his diary or memoirs or autobiography. Why do you suppose he identifies

the sections in this way? On p. 144 he refers to 'the prehistoric days'. Define his idea of history and prehistory and work out what this means to him and why.

Focus on: dreams and roses

LOOK OVER AND COLLECT . . .
— Charles relates several of his dreams to us during this chapter. Collect them all together as related episodes and see what sense you make of them as a group.
— Then do the same with all the references to roses in this chapter. What symbolic meaning might be attached to them and why are they being used here? How might the dreams and the roses interconnect?

PART II, HISTORY THREE
(pp. 153–238)

Focus on: place and distance

DECIDE ON THE EFFECT . . .
— Charles tells us at the beginning of this chapter that, in fact, he is now in London, and has been writing in London, not at Shruff End, ever since p. 100. Ask yourself again what this suggests about his perspective on the events that he relates. How much do you trust his narrative of the events?

Focus on: marriage

ASSESS . . .
— 'Every persisting marriage is based on fear,' Peregrine had said (p. 153). (Or did he? Later on you will see that Peregrine denies saying something that Charles had reported to us. Look out for that and note the implications.)

— Think about the relevance of this statement to the circumstances portrayed in this novel. Why are there so many statements and clichés about marriage? How does that fact connect to the story and the moral of the story being told here? Collect some such proverbs and quotations to help you. Here are a few to get you going:

- 'Marriage has many pains, but celibacy has no pleasures.' Samuel Johnson, *Rasselas* (1759)
- 'Marriage is a bribe to make a housekeeper think she's a house-holder.' Thornton Wilder, *The Merchant of Yonkers* (1939)
- 'Marriage is like life in this – that it is a field of battle, and not a bed of roses.' Robert Louis Stevenson, *Virginibus Puerisque* (1881)
- 'Marriage is a wonderful invention; but, then again, so is a bicycle repair kit.' Billy Connolly.

Focus on: the sea monster

COMPARE AND CONTRAST . . .
— Charles looks at Titian's picture of Perseus and Andromeda in the art gallery at the Wallace Collection. He does and does not connect this image with his vision of the sea monster (p. 171). Then he looks at Rembrandt's 'Titus'. What does this net of images suggest? If you do not know the story of Perseus then look it up in a dictionary of classical mythology. Remember that Charles's major preoccupation now is 'rescuing' Hartley. Work out the relevance of this theme in relation to this scene.

Focus on: James

CONSIDER CAREFULLY AND CRITICALLY EVALUATE . . .
— Look at the description of James's flat that begins on p. 172. How does this compare with the houses that we have

already encountered in the novel – Shruff End, Nibletts, Charles's London flat?

— Then look at Charles's description of James's appearance (pp. 173–4). How does this help to place him?

— 'The sea, the sea, yes' (p. 176) it is *James* who utters the title of the book. What does this suggest? In order to help you focus on this question, disentangle all the stuff that Charles says and thinks here, from what James is saying. What kinds of philosophical points of view is James offering? (Try to ignore Charles for a while.)

ASK YOURSELF . . .

— James says, '. . . you may be deluding yourself in thinking that you have really loved this woman all these years' (p. 178). What do you think?

Focus on: first love

NOTE AND COMPARE . . .

— Several characters discuss the importance of first love in this chapter. Collect all the references you can and see if a pattern of analysis is emerging.

Focus on: the theatre and the theatrical

EVALUATE . . .

— Charles overhears Ben and Mary (pp. 195–9). He says, 'It will be clear who is speaking.' How far is he setting himself up as the 'theatre director' here?

AND TRANSFORM . . .

— Rewrite this scene from Mary or Ben's point of view, in the first person. How differently does that make you react to the characters?

Focus on: narrative

NOTE AGAIN . . .
— 'I will now describe what happened next, much of which was entirely unexpected' (p. 207). How does this fit with Charles's narrative patterns in the storytelling so far?

Focus on: the kiss

FIND OTHER REFERENCES . . .
— Charles tells us that when he kissed Hartley it 'transformed' her, as in the fairy tales. Seek out such references: think of *Sleeping Beauty*, or *Beauty and the Beast*, or *The Frog Prince*. How many others can you find? And what about in literature? What is the symbolic meaning of the first kiss, and why does it matter so much, do you suppose?

PART II, FOUR
(pp. 239–341)

Focus on: narrative and storytelling

NOTE AGAIN . . .
— 'What follows this, and also what directly precedes it, has been written at a much later date' (p. 239). Keep thinking about perspective and timing, and keep assessing your own critical views on Charles's veracity.

WHAT KIND OF STORY? . . .
— Look at p. 243 where Charles explains the way in which his strange household settles into a routine. 'Thus, for a brief time, we lived together, each absorbed in his own illusions, and together we regressed into a life of primal simplicity and almost fetishistic private obsession.'

— What kinds of story might this remind you of? Think about Daniel Defoe's *Robinson Crusoe*, William Golding's *The Lord of the Flies*, Enid Blyton's 'Famous Five' series, R. M. Ballantyne's *Coral Island*. In what ways might any of these books offer a useful comparison for what is going on at Shruff End at this point?

Focus on: the title

WHAT DOES IT SUGGEST? . . .

— When Charles meets Titus, the boy says, 'Oh, the sea, the sea – it's so wonderful' (p. 251). James has said the title; now Titus is given the words too. What does this suggest?

Focus on: Hartley

CRITICALLY ASSESS . . .

— On p. 255 Titus says that Hartley is 'a bit of an imaginer, a fantasist, I suppose most women are'. Assess this statement in the light of your own opinions of Charles – and Hartley – so far.

Focus on: the theatre

QUESTION . . .

— Charles says on p. 272 that he pursues 'the role that I had adopted'. What role do you suppose this to be, and is this, in your opinion, a good or a bad thing?

Focus on: symbols and meanings

LOOK OVER AND COLLECT . . .

— As you go on with this chapter look for meaningful symbols. In particular work out the significance of:

- The idea of the princess
- Olives

- Dreams
- Fantasy and fantasists
- Children
- The internal room
- Food
- Singing
- The camping-out scene (look at p. 327)

PART II, FIVE
(pp. 343–88)

Focus on: storytelling

NOTE AND RECALL . . .

— 'The next day was one of the worst days of my life, perhaps the worst' (p. 343). How does this make you react? How far do you feel that you are being manipulated by Charles's narrative?

Focus on: symbols

ASSESS . . .

— In his account of his parting from Hartley, Charles uses a number of images associated with weddings. Note these down and consider how they contribute to Charles's attitudes to Hartley and his relation to Hartley.

MAKE CONNECTIONS . . .

— When the deputation arrives at Nibletts there are several bowls of dead roses (p. 347). What does this suggest?

Focus on: the crisis

CONSIDER . . .

— On p. 365 Charles begins to tell of the events surrounding and following on from his near drowning. Consider how this might relate to other images and scenes that have already passed in the novel. Also ask yourself about the ways in which this episode may bring about the beginning of a kind of transformation for Charles. In the Contexts section you will find some suggestions of other novels and works where the imagery of water or drowning – or both – leads to some significant crisis.

Focus on: James

PONDER . . .
— What do you think has happened to James? Look at pp. 382–3. Then look up the story about Christ and the woman with a haemorrhage in the New Testament Mark chapter 5 verses 25–34. Can you make any connections and, if so, what might these connections suggest about James?

AND AGAIN . . .
— The conversation with James ends when Lizzie screams (p. 386). Why do you suppose that these events are so closely juxtaposed? It is just 'accidental' of course, but remember that nothing in a novel is 'just' accidental.

Focus on: Titus

LET YOURSELF IMAGINE . . .
— Write a list of all the things that Titus represented to all the people present. What did he mean to Hartley, Ben, Charles, Lizzie, Gilbert, James, Perry, Rosina?
— Titus is the only young person who has figured in the novel so far. Why might that be important? In fact, there is one other young person – can you work out who this is?
— Then look over these statements and consider which you think to be most relevant and important to a reading of the novel as a whole. Rank them in order.

- Titus's death is the central tragedy of *The Sea, The Sea.*
- Charles is responsible for Titus's death.
- Titus has to be sacrificed.
- Hartley is released by Titus's death.
- James let Titus die.

PART II, SIX
(pp. 389–476)

Focus on: the aftermath

LOOK UP THEN CONSIDER . . .

— Look up the word 'aftermath' in a dictionary. Strictly speaking, it is an old farming term to do with the harvest. How does that definition relate to what is going on here? Consider the ways in which all the different characters react to Titus's death. If you take the proverb 'No loss without some gain', what 'gain' can you see for any of these characters in Titus's death?

— Why – in the symbolic and metaphoric terms of the novel – does Titus have to die *by drowning*?

Focus on: Ben and Mary

LOOK BACK . . .

— On pp. 418–25 Charles goes again to visit Ben and Mary Fitch. Look back at the last episode of this kind on pp. 122–8. What has changed? Who is in charge in this episode, as opposed to the last?

Focus on: James

WEIGH UP . . .

— James comes back again (p. 440). Read over the resulting discussion carefully and consider James's relation to Charles.

On p. 441 James says 'What larks we had'. This is (or may be) a quotation from Charles Dickens's *Great Expectations* (1861) where Joe Gargery, bringing up his wife's much younger brother Pip, shares a conspiracy of pleasure and release with the boy, 'What larks!' If you are familiar with *Great Expectations*, you might like to think about how the relation between Pip and Joe might parallel the relation between Charles and James.

Focus on: letters

CONSIDER . . .

— On pp. 462–4 we are given the texts of a group of letters received by Charles. Letters have figured throughout the whole novel, but what do these suggest? We have not met Rosemary, we have barely met Angela. Why do you suppose that they appear now?

Focus on: The Tempest

CONSIDER AND ASSESS . . .

— Now that you have almost read the whole novel, think again about the 'intertext' of Shakespeare's *The Tempest*. (It is mentioned again on p. 399.) Might it be possible to make parallels with the various characters in each work? How far can you take such an interpretation? For instance, would you agree or disagree with this suggested list of parallels?

- Charles as Prospero
- Lizzie as Ariel
- Titus as Ferdinand
- Ben as Prospero's usurping brother
- Hartley as Miranda
- Gilbert Opian as Caliban

— There is nothing hard and fast about these suggestions. As you will see from the section in this guide entitled Interviews and Silences, Murdoch herself both acknowledged the influence of *The Tempest* and refused to see it as in any way systematic. All that you are doing is playing with possibilities as a way of opening up the text to interpretation.

Focus on: the horrible thing

LOOK BACK . . .

— Charles's narrative began with the mention of something 'so extraordinary and so horrible that I cannot bring myself to describe it even now' (p. 1). He then told the reader what that horrible thing was on pp. 18–21. On p. 466 the sea serpent returns again. Now that you have read the whole of Charles's narrative about what happened at Shruff End – that is, while he was living by the sea – consider this vision (or whatever it was) again. How many times has it returned in the course of the story? Look over the novel and find specific examples. At the beginning you were asked to assess what the vision might mean – literally, practically, metaphorically and psychologically. Ask yourself the same question again now, bearing in mind all the different occasions where it is mentioned. Is your answer different now from first time around?

AND CONNECT . . .

— On p. 476 Charles tells us about the seals that he sees in the early morning. How might that vision connect to his early vision of the 'sea monster'?

Looking over Part II

QUESTIONS FOR DISCUSSION OR ESSAYS

1. Titus says Hartley is a 'fantasist'. Do you agree?

2. Assess Titus's role in the novel as a whole.

3. Consider the importance of ANY TWO of these characters in the novel so far: Gilbert, Rosina, Freddie Arkwright, Ben, Angela, Peregrine.

4. 'James is the central pivot in *The Sea, The Sea*. Only he can teach Charles the lessons he has to learn.' Discuss.

5. Compare and contrast the houses in *The Sea, The Sea*.

PART III, POSTSCRIPT
(pp. 477–502)

Focus on: storytelling

LOOK BACK AND COMPARE . . .
— This section is quite different from those that precede it, in that the 'entries' are, for the most part, considerably shorter and more immediate. Consider what this suggests about Charles's new attitudes to life and his priorities.

Focus on: magic

INTERPRET . . .
— Charles says, 'I was the dreamer, I the magician' (p. 499). How do you interpret this?

Focus on: what next?

LOOK AGAIN AT THE TITLE . . .
— Read the last words of the novel. Think again about the title of the book. You might also like to look at the Contexts section to consider the suggestions there about the allusions contained in the title.

CONSIDER . . .
— Why do you suppose Charles is going to meet Angela for lunch (p. 501)?

Looking over the whole novel

QUESTIONS FOR DISCUSSION OR ESSAYS

1. 'The end of *The Sea, The Sea* takes us back to the beginning.' Discuss.

2. 'The most important question in this novel is "Who is one's first love?"' Discuss.

3. Analyse the imagery associated with water and the sea in this novel.

4. Consider the use Murdoch makes of allusions to *The Tempest* in *The Sea, The Sea*.

5. What is the role of magic in *The Sea, The Sea*?

6. 'All the women in *The Sea, The Sea* are nothing but ciphers.' Discuss.

7. 'James is the most important character in the novel.' Discuss.

8. How do the terms and characters of fairy tales colour events and attitudes in *The Sea, The Sea*?

Contexts, comparisons and complementary readings

These sections suggest contextual and comparative ways of reading these three novels by Murdoch. You can put your reading in a social, historical or literary context. You can make comparisons – again, social, literary or historical – with other texts or art works. Or you can choose complementary works (of whatever kind) – that is, art works, literary works, social reportage or facts which in some way illuminate the text by sidelights or interventions which you can make into a telling framework. Some of the suggested contexts are directly connected to the book, in that they will give you precise literary or social frames in which to situate the novel. In turn, these are either related to the period within which the novel is set, or to the time – now – when you are reading it. Some of these examples are designed to suggest books or other texts that may make useful sources for comparison (or for complementary purposes) when you are reading *The Sea, The Sea*. Again, they may be related to literary or critical themes, or they may be relevant to social and cultural themes current 'then' or 'now'.

Focus on: the sea

THINK ABOUT THE TITLE . . .

While you were reading this novel you were considering the impact and relevance of the title. Peter Conradi points out in his book on Murdoch's work, *The Saint and the Artist: A Study of the Fiction of Iris Murdoch* (1986), that there are two clear references that lie behind this title. The first of these is '*thalassa, thalassa*' from the Greek of Xenophon's *Anabasis* which is set during the Persian wars. At this moment the weary Greek warriors catch sight of the sea and cry out with delight because to have arrived at the sea means that they will soon be embarking for home. The second, which alludes to the first, is from the French poet Paul Valéry's poem 'The Graveyard by the Sea' which is about 'escape from and return to the world' and has as its final line, '*La mer, la mer, toujours recommencée*' – 'The sea, the sea, everything begins again'.

— Consider the implications of these references. What connections can you make to the circumstances or the plot or the characters in Murdoch's novel? Note that if the book were simply called *The Sea*, rather than *The Sea, The Sea*, you might not imagine that there was any allusion in the title at all.

BRAINSTORM . . .

— Think about water generally and about the sea in particular. How many associations can you think of that traditionally go with our ideas of water and the sea?
— You might think of the book of Genesis in the Old Testament where life begins in the formless ocean. Modern evolution theory also draws on the sea as the origin of life on earth. Water is essential for all forms of life. Human beings are composed more of water than anything else. The child in the womb is encased in amniotic fluid. Water is the fountain of

life and rebirth. Christian and other religious baptism ceremonies employ the symbol of water. Without water there is desert, and yet water – and the sea – can also be associated with drowning and destruction.

— Consider other famous books about the sea or which use the symbolism of water – in terms of drowning and purging and re-affirming – such as: Shakespeare's *The Tempest*, T. S. Eliot's poem *The Waste Land*, Margaret Atwood's *Surfacing*, George Eliot's *The Mill on the Floss*, Charles Dickens's *David Copperfield*, Samuel Taylor Coleridge's poem 'The Rime of the Ancient Mariner', Matthew Arnold's poem 'Dover Beach', Herman Melville's *Moby-Dick*. If you look at the Interviews and Silences section at the beginning of this book, you will see that Murdoch herself sees water imagery in all her novels. *The Bell* might make a useful comparison for *The Sea, The Sea*, as would *Nuns and Soldiers*.

Focus on: Buddhism

LOOK UP . . .
— When John Haffenden interviewed Murdoch for his collection *Novelists in Interview* (1985), they discussed the question of Buddhism and her ideas about its terms and the application of those terms in her novels. She said:

> It seems to me that some kind of Christian
> Buddhism would make a satisfactory religion . . .
> Buddhism is a good picture of the thing – not, of
> course, its mythical ideas about reincarnation, but
> that the aim is to destroy the ego. Schopenhauer
> plays with this idea, that one's task in life is to be
> aware of the world without the ego. It's not at all an
> other-worldly religion, its absolutely this-worldly,

here and now: this is where it's all happening and there isn't anywhere else. But to deny the ego is the most difficult thing of all.

— Murdoch says many other things on this subject and you might like to look up that interview in Haffenden's book.

Focus on: first love

MAKE ASSOCIATIONS . . .
— *The Sea, The Sea* seems to be about Charles's 'first love', Hartley. But he asks himself the question of who is one's 'first love' at the end of the novel. There is some suggestion that this, after all, may be James. It's also a question that Charles asks of others during the course of the novel. Ask yourself about 'first love'. What might its significance be? Why do you suppose it has such significance in Western culture? Why is it the subject of so many plays, films, novels? Is it the experience itself that is important? Or the memory of the experience? Here are some quotations to help you focus your consideration:

- 'I have somewhat against thee, because thou hast left thy first love.' New Testament, Revelation, chapter 2, verse 4
- 'When I was a child, I/ loved a pumping-engine,/ thought it every bit/ as beautiful as you.' W. H. Auden ('Heavy Date' 1939 p. 153)
- 'Dear as remembered kisses after death,
  And sweet as those by hopeless fancy feigned
  On lips that are for others; deep as love,
  Deep as first love, and wild with all regret;
  O Death in Life, the days that are no more.'
Alfred, Lord Tennyson, *The Princess*, (1847) Part 4

Focus on: courtly love

— Some of Charles's attitudes to and ideas about Hartley –
and his memory of his love for Hartley – are based on a version
of the medieval idea of courtly love. His utter belief (against
all the evidence) that she returns his love is a perversion of this
ideal. Find out about courtly love. You could refer to Chaucer's
Book of the Duchess as an example of this convention, or Malory's
Morte D'Arthur. Then look at some of the more modern texts
that take up and rework similar ideas. These might include:
Tennyson's *Idylls of the King*, Dickens's *Great Expectations*, John
Fowles's *The Collector*, Wagner's opera *Tristan and Isolde* and
Alfred Hitchcock's film *Vertigo*.

VINTAGE
LIVING
TEXTS

Reference

Selected extracts from critical works

These brief extracts from critical articles on Murdoch's work are designed to be used to suggest angles on the text that may be relevant to the themes of the books, their settings, their literary methods, their historical contexts, or to indicate their relevance to issues, questions or problems today.

Sometimes one critic's opinion will be entirely contradicted by another's. You might use these passages to ask yourself whether or not you agree with the writer's assessments. Or else you might take phrases from these articles to use for framing questions – for discussion, or for essays – about the texts.

None of these critical opinions are the last word. They are simply contributions to a cultural debate. As such, they should be approached with intellectual interest and intelligent assessment. But in the end, it is your own reading of a text that really counts.

Peter J. Conradi
From *The Saint and the Artist: A Study of the Fiction of Iris Murdoch*
On literary allusion and the map in *The Bell*

The necessary connections between sex and virtue form part of the backdrop to the works. The scenery of *The Bell* is borrowed from the *Phaedo* [a Dialogue by the ancient Greek philosopher Plato], with its four rivers and its insistence that the proper study of philosophy is dying, though the lake, causeway, ferry and circles may also owe something to Dante's *Inferno* [the first part of his *Divine Comedy*]. An aerial map of Imber would show three sets of walls, and resemble a dartboard. The outer circle is the wall of half-stripped Imber Court, the next the wall of the wholly austere Abbey, and the last of the three concentric rings, the *hortus conclusus* [enclosed garden] containing the happy cemetery with its laughing nuns. It is a Platonic map of degrees of unselfing. Only Toby penetrates by mistake to the centre, and in fact no gate is locked. That this spiritual symmetry does not obtrude may have something to do with the fact that 'the religious symbols and institutions involved are both established and discredited in our minds'. The map seems a public one.

A. S. Byatt
From *Degrees of Freedom: The Early Novels of
Iris Murdoch*
On the symbolism of 'the bell'

I think that the bell certainly connects with the
solidity of the normal, with the unutterably particular mystery; it is surely significant in this context
that it is made, by a playful cross-reference not
unique in Miss Murdoch's work, to have been built
by 'a great craftsman at Gloucester, Hugh Belleyetere
or Bellfounder' and it resembles Hugo, when it is
dragged up from the depths in that it is seen as
something 'enormous', 'monstrous', 'a thing from
another world'. But the two bells, the old and the
new, carry further associations in the novel.

James sees the bell as a symbol for purity, clarity,
candour, and compares it explicitly with Catherine
Fawley, who is seen as having these qualities by the
other characters, and who, like the bell, will enter
the Abbey as a postulant. But Catherine has her
twin, Nicholas, whom James sees as a disruptive
force, and the new bell has its twin, buried in the
mud of the lake. The old bell is, through its history,
associated with violent and disruptive passion, with
sin and confession; its legend is, appropriately, *Vox
ego Amoris sum* . . . In this sense it helps to
symbolize the ambiguity of love in the novel, where
love is both a dangerous loss of purity and exercise
of power, and a necessary part of humanity. And
Nick's destruction of the second bell, the postulant,
destroys his sister, who, like the nun, runs into the
lake to drown herself, seeing herself as corrupt
because she, as Nicholas has done, loves Michael.

Both Michael and James use the bell as a symbol for man's spiritual nature in their sermons; James is attracted by the idea of its simplicity, the way in which it must speak out clearly if moved; Michael uses it as a symbol for man's spiritual energy.

Candia McWilliam
From the introduction to the Vintage edition of
The Black Prince
On clothes

I have always relished this novelist on clothes: vatic, hieratic, Shakespearean, *travesti*, Mannerist, fairytale, seven league, old masterly, heraldic, the garments come from her head, transformative and magical and extravagant as *haute couture* itself (though she will treat a humble mac to the same glow), with no nod to the unfledged stuffs dependent from hangers most of us keep in our cupboards. Creative energy, a kind of exalted drive, and a quality perhaps most closely definable as innocence keep Dame Iris's descriptions of clothing, as of children and the young, from being at odds with her great themes, or, simply, beyond belief.

Candia McWilliam
From the introduction to the Vintage edition of
The Black Prince
On Julian's role in *The Black Prince*

Julian Baffin is as ambiguous to look at as is her name, and she, crucially, dresses as the hero of the play by which she is possessed, *Hamlet*, at one of the plot's crises. At other times she recalls a timid deer, a lion, a fox. She is the herald of romance and also of danger. Our view of her good faith fluctuates. Is she manipulative or innocent, delinquent and destructive or just young; and is not to be young to be all of the foregoing? As in other novels by Iris Murdoch, the vocabulary of the young is touchingly unmimetic; very few young women of the Seventies, when Julian Baffin came to be and, presumably, is living, used the words 'absurd' or 'I say'. Yet these idioms roost quite easily in the branches of Iris Murdoch's stout yet airy novels. Perhaps it has to do with her lack of false dignity as an artist, the absence of a constructed personality lying against the grain of her nature.

Peter J. Conradi
From *The Saint and the Artist: A Study of the Fiction of Iris Murdoch*
On *Hamlet* in *The Black Prince*

The analogy which *The Black Prince* proposes between itself and *Hamlet* – made explicit in Bradley's seminar to Julian – is that both texts invite and require a Freudian reading, and neither can be satisfied or exhausted by it. Like the Post Office Tower, which so dominates this novel, both *Hamlet* and *The Black Prince* exemplify an Eros both Freudian and also Platonic. 'And every man in London is obsessed with the Post Office Tower' argues Bradley, demythologising the merely Freudian content of the symbol.

Thus we come to Bradley's seminar on *Hamlet* with Julian. Murdoch's interest in the Oedipus conflict in many of the novels has been noted. What is striking about Bradley's discussion is that, first of all, he begins with a brilliant and succinct précis of Ernest Jones's Freudian reading of the play, and then suggests the qualified relevance of such a reading to the sophisticated reader. [He quotes p. 197 of *The Black Prince* from 'Shut up' to 'You are a sophisticated reader *in ovo*'.]

'Ma and pa' nicely domesticates *Hamlet* and brings it closer to Ealing, but 'It is true but it doesn't matter' is, in a sense, precisely what the novel invites us to feel about its own Oedipal or family romance. Arnold clearly loves his daughter to a degree that Bradley's love-affair with her strikes him as 'criminal', 'a defilement', since it is an acting-out of his own unconscious wishes. There is similarly an element within Julian's love for Bradley which is a deferment of her love for her father, an expression through a (just) permissible surrogate of what would otherwise be taboo.

Hilda Spear
From *Iris Murdoch*
On the role of James in *The Sea, The Sea*

The moral weight of *The Sea, The Sea* rests on James; he . . . is the saint, though . . . he does not have to battle against a truly demonic figure and his powers of goodness appear to embrace magic. On his last visit to Charles at Shruff End he seems to pave the way for his own death, not only by clearing up all earthly misunderstandings, but also by hinting at the 'journey' he is about to take. It is on this final visit that the most serious discussion in the novel on the question of goodness and religion takes place: 'Goodness', he tells Charles, 'is giving up power and acting upon the world negatively.' It is perhaps a message for Charles, who despite his apparent with-drawal from the world, has attempted to hold on to his power over his friends and over events; simulta-neously, however, it is a statement of James's own intentions: 'The last achievement is the absolute surrender of magic itself, the end of what you call superstition.' He is himself undergoing that process of surrendering everything.

Peter J Conradi
From *The Saint and the Artist: A Study of the Fiction of Iris Murdoch*
On the role of James in *The Sea, The Sea*

One clue as to James's real feelings for Charles occurs early in Part 5 [of Part II, History]. They are discussing Charles's feelings for Hartley, whose return to Ben James has successfully negotiated. Charles is still full of illusion about her [quotes pp. 354–5].

The irony of this conversation is that James, whose deepest affections seem to be for his own sex, clearly feels connected to Charles in something approximating to the way that Charles feels connected to Hartley. He makes Charles his sole heir. Just as Charles recalls every detail of his rela-tions with Hartley – or is haunted by those details he can recall – so James is repeatedly shown recalling

Charles as a child. He remembers throwing stones with Charles, remembers that Charles liked black beetles, demonstrates the sense of connection he feels for Charles in a variety of ways. He pockets the hammer Charles is mending, intuiting that he means no good by it. In a sense he nurses him.

Glossary of literary terms

Allusion A self-conscious reference to some other literary text, symbol, history or fact. In everyday speech '9/11' is now an 'allusion' which we all agree to understand in terms of our memory of an historical event. But 'once more unto the breach' is also an allusion to Shakespeare's *Henry V*.

Analogon A noun derived from 'analogy'. A person or idea is 'analogous' with something else, and can be compared with and be shown to be similar.

Chronology The order of events as they actually take place in time. This might also be called a 'time-line'. It is opposed to the order of events as they are told – which may be inverted or muddled up in many ways with flashbacks and looking ahead, etc.

Comedy Strictly speaking, the opposite to 'tragedy'. In contemporary life this often refers to a literary work that seeks to amuse its audience. In classical terms, it means any story or work of art that resolves itself and has a 'happy' ending.

Denouement From the French, meaning the 'denuding' or revelation – usually at the conclusion where the twists and turns of the plot are explained. For example, at the end of *Othello*, the *denouement* is Desdemona's murder and the revelation of Iago's deception.

Imagery Any set of recurring ideas or themes that can be put together to make a pattern or net of connections.

Intertextuality Where one text uses or exploits another text. Tom Stoppard's play *Rosencrantz and Guildenstern are Dead* exploits an intertextuality with Shakespeare's *Hamlet* in that the events of the original play are assumed to be taking place offstage.

Irony A subtle method of conveying some counterpoint or inconsistency which may be humorous or sad.

Liminality To be on the threshold, or at the border, neither one thing nor the other. Charlotte Brontës *Jane Eyre* (1847) opens with Jane enclosed between the window and the curtains, neither inside nor outside, and she spends much of the text in similar 'liminal' situations.

Melodrama Literally, a drama accompanied by music. In ancient Greece it was simply that, but the nineteenth-century fashion for playing dramatic music to go with sensational plays about murder and horror means that the term has come to mean anything 'over the top'.

Metaphor Any figure of speech by which one thing is explained or described by relating it to some other thing. It splits into two elements: the 'tenor' which is the primary subject, and the 'vehicle' which is the secondary figurative term applied to it. For instance, in 'the whirligig of time', 'time' is the 'tenor' or the primary subject because the metaphor is designed to tell us something about the nature of time, and the 'whirligig' is the 'vehicle' because it is the image or figure designed to show what time is like – i.e. it brings everything back round again.

Myth A narrative with an unknown origin that has been passed on through the centuries orally, and which attempts to explain some essential feature of human life – whether religious belief, or the origin of life.

Sensation literature Any work designed specifically to make the audience react emotionally – especially to feel shock. Examples include the novels of Wilkie Collins, *The Woman in White* for instance, also those of Mary Braddon, such as *Lady Audley's Secret*, and the plays of Arthur Wing Pinero, such as *The Second Mrs Tanqueray*. The plots for such works are liable to include bigamy, sexual misdeed, murder, deception and madness.

Tragedy A fiction or drama that traces the downfall of a protagonist who is often portrayed as being more able or gifted than others. The 'tragedy' is often some fall from grace brought about by an accident, an error in judgement or by a cruel twist of fate. Often the catalyst is some 'tragic flaw' in the character of the hero, such as Macbeth's gullibility and ambition.

Biographical outline

1919 Iris Murdoch born in Dublin.

1920 Family moved to London where her father worked in the Civil Service.

1931–8 Boarded at Badminton School.

1938–42 Studied Greats at Somerville College, Oxford.

1942–4 Joined the Civil Service as an assistant principal in the Treasury.

1944–6 Worked in Europe as an administrative officer for United Nations Relief and Rehabilitation Services.

1947–8 Held a Sarah Smithson Studentship in philosophy at Newnham College, Cambridge.

1948 Appointed Lecturer in Philosophy and Fellow at St Anne's College, Oxford.

1953 *Sartre: Romantic Rationalist* published.

1954 *Under the Net* published.

1956 *The Flight from the Enchanter* published.

1957 *The Sandcastle* published.

1958 *The Bell* published.

1961 *A Severed Head* published.

1962 *An Unofficial Rose* published.

1963 Named Honorary Fellow of St Anne's College, Oxford. *The Unicorn* published.

1963–7 Lecturer at the Royal College of Art, London.

1964 *The Italian Girl* published.

1965 *The Red and the Green* published.

1966 *The Time of the Angels* published.

1968 *The Nice and the Good* published.

1969 *Bruno's Dream* published.

1970 *The Sovereignty of Good* and *A Fairly Honourable Defeat* published.

1971 *An Accidental Man* published.

1973 *The Black Prince* published. Awarded the James Tait Black Memorial Prize.

1974 *The Sacred and Profane Love Machine* published. Awarded the Whitbread Prize.

1975 *A Word Child* published

1976 Awarded the CBE. *Henry and Cato* published. Delivered the Romanes Lectures.

1977 *The Fire and the Sun: Why Plato Banished the Artists* published.

1978 *The Sea, The Sea* published. Awarded the Booker Prize.

1980 *Nuns and Soldiers* published. *Art and Eros*, a Platonic Dialogue on some themes from *The Fire and the Sun*, produced for platform performance at the National Theatre.

1982 Delivered the Gifford Lectures in Natural Theology at the University of Edinburgh, entitled 'Metaphysics as a Guide to Morals'.

1983 *The Philosopher's Pupil* published.

1985 *The Good Apprentice* published.

1986 *Acastos: Two Platonic Dialogues* published.

1987 Created a Dame of the British Empire. *The Book and the Brotherhood* published.

1989 *The Message to the Planet* published.

1992 *Metaphysics as a Guide to Morals* published.

1993 *The Green Knight* published.
1995 *Jackson's Dilemma* published.
1999 Died in Oxford.

Select bibliography

NOVELS BY IRIS MURDOCH

Under the Net (Chatto & Windus, London, 1954; Vintage London, 2002)

The Flight from the Enchanter (Chatto & Windus, 1956; Vintage, 2000)

The Sandcastle (Chatto & Windus, 1957; Vintage, 2003)

The Bell (Chatto & Windus, 1958; Vintage, 1999)

A Severed Head (Chatto & Windus, 1961; Vintage, 2001)

An Unofficial Rose (Chatto & Windus, 1962; Vintage, 2001)

The Unicorn (Chatto & Windus, 1963; Vintage, 2001)

The Italian Girl (Chatto & Windus, 1964; Vintage, 2003)

The Red and the Green (Chatto & Windus, 1965; Vintage, 2002)

The Time of the Angels (Chatto & Windus, 1966; Vintage, 2002)

The Nice and the Good (Chatto & Windus, 1968; Vintage, 2000)

Bruno's Dream (Chatto & Windus, 1969; Vintage, 2001)

A Fairly Honourable Defeat (Chatto & Windus, 1970; Vintage, 2002)

An Accidental Man (Chatto & Windus, 1971; Vintage, 2003)

The Black Prince (Chatto & Windus, 1973; Vintage, 1999)

The Sacred and Profane Love Machine (Chatto & Windus, 1974; Vintage, 2003)

A Word Child (Chatto & Windus, 1975; Vintage, 2002)

Henry and Cato (Chatto & Windus, 1976; Vintage, 2002)

The Sea, The Sea (Chatto & Windus, 1978; Vintage, 1999)

Nuns and Soldiers (Chatto & Windus, 1980; Vintage, 2001)
The Philosopher's Pupil (Chatto & Windus, 1983; Vintage, 2000)
The Good Apprentice (Chatto & Windus, 1985; Vintage, 2000)
The Book and the Brotherhood (Chatto & Windus, 1987; Vintage, 2003)
The Message to the Planet (Chatto & Windus, 1989; Vintage, 1999)
The Green Knight (Chatto & Windus, 1993)
Jackson's Dilemma (Chatto & Windus, 1995)

SHORT STORY
'Something Special', *Winters Tales* III (London, 1957), pp. 175–204 (reissued, Vintage, 1999)

NON-FICTION
Sartre: Romantic Rationalist (Bowes & Bowes, Cambridge 1953; reissued with new introduction, 1987)
'Philosophy and Beliefs', in *Twentieth Century* (June 1955), pp. 495–521
'Metaphysics and Ethics', in D. F. Pears, ed., *The Nature of Metaphysics* (Macmillan & Co., London, 1957)
'The Sublime and the Beautiful Revisited', in *Yale Review*, XLIX (Winter, 1959), pp. 247–71
'Against Dryness: A Polemical Essay', in *Encounter* XVI (January 1961), pp. 16–20; reprinted in Malcolm Bradbury, ed., *The Novel Today* (Fontana, Glasgow, 1977), pp. 23–31
The Sovereignty of Good (Routledge & Kegan Paul, London, 1970)
The Fire and the Sun: Why Plato Banished the Artists (Clarendon Press, Oxford, 1977)
Metaphysics as a Guide to Morals (Chatto & Windus, London, 1992)
Existentialists and Mystics: Writings on Philosophy and Literature, Peter J. Conradi, ed. (Chatto & Windus, London, 1997)
Occasional Essays by Iris Murdoch, Yozo Muroya and Paul Hullah, eds (Okayama, 1998)

PLAYS

Iris Murdoch and J. B. Priestley, *A Severed Head* (Samuel French, London, 1964)

James Saunders and Iris Murdoch, *The Italian Girl* (London, 1968)

The Three Arrows with *The Servants and the Snow* (Chatto & Windus, London, 1973)

The Servants, libretto for opera by William Mathias (Oxford University Press, London, 1980)

Acastos: Two Platonic Dialogues (Penguin, London, 1986)

The Black Prince (Samuel French, London, 1989)

Joanna, Joanna, radio play broadcast on BBC Radio 3, February 1987 (Colophon with Old Town, London, 1994)

A Year of Birds, symphonic song cycle with music by Malcolm Williamson (1995)

POETRY

A Year of Birds, with engravings by Reynolds Stone (Tisbury, Wiltshire, 1978; revised edition 1984)

Four poems in *Poetry London Apple Magazine* I, 1 (Autumn, 1979), pp. 38–42

'Miss Beatrice May Baker', in *People: Essays and Poems*, Susan Hill, ed. (Chatto & Windus London, 1983), pp. 114–15

Poems by Iris Murdoch, Yozo Muroya and Paul Hullah, eds (Okayama, 1997)

INTERVIEWS

Michael Bellamy, 'An Interview with Iris Murdoch', *Contemporary Literature*, XVIII (1977), pp. 129–40

C.W.E. Bigsby, in H. Ziegler and C.W.E. Bigsby, eds, *The Radical Imagination and the Liberal Tradition: Interviews with English and American Novelists* (Junction Books, London, 1982), pp. 209–30

Jack Biles, 'An Interview with Iris Murdoch', *Studies in the Literary Imagination*, XI (Fall, 1978), pp. 115–25

Gillian Dooley, *Conversations with Iris Murdoch* (University of South Carolina Press, Columbia, 1989).

John Haffenden, 'John Haffenden talks to Iris Murdoch', *Literary Review*, LVIII (April 1983), pp. 31–5

John Haffenden, ed., *Novelists in Interview* (Methuen, London, 1985), pp. 191–209

Frank Kermode, 'House of Fiction: Interviews with Seven English Novelists', *Partisan Review*, XXX (1963), pp. 61–83

Ronald Lello, ed., *Revelations: Glimpses of Reality* (Shepheard–Walwyn, London, 1985), pp. 82–90

BIBLIOGRAPHY AND BIOGRAPHY

John Bayley, *Iris: A Memoir of Iris Murdoch* (Duckworth, London, 1998; Abacus, London, 2000).

Peter J. Conradi, *Iris Murdoch: A Life* (HarperCollins, London, 2001).

John Fletcher and Cheryl Bove, eds, *Iris Murdoch: A Descriptive Primary and Annotated Secondary Bibliography* (Garland, London and New York, 1994).

Thomas I. Tominaga and Wilma Scheidermeyer, *Iris Murdoch and Muriel Spark: A Bibliography* (Scarecrow Press, Metuchen, New Jersey, 1976).

CRITICISM

M. Antonaccio, *Picturing the Human: The Moral Thought of Iris Murdoch* (Oxford University Press, Oxford, 2000).

M. Antonaccio and W. Schweiker, eds, *Iris Murdoch and the Search for Human Goodness* (Chicago University Press, Chicago, 1996).

Frank Baldanza, *Iris Murdoch* (Twayne Publishers, New York, 1974).

Kate Begnal, *Iris Murdoch: A Reference Guide* (G. K. Hall, Boston, Mass., 1987).

Harold Bloom, ed., *Iris Murdoch: Modern Critical Views* (Chelsea House, New York, 1986).

Cheryl Bove, *Character Index and Guide to the Fiction of Iris Murdoch* (Garland, New York, 1986).

Cheryl Bove, *Understanding Iris Murdoch* (University of South Carolina Press, Columbia, 1993).

Malcolm Bradbury, '"A House Fit for Free Characters": Iris Murdoch and *Under the Net*', in *Possibilities: Essays on the State of the Novel* (London, 1973).

A. S. Byatt, *Degrees of Freedom: The Early Novels of Iris Murdoch* (Chatto & Windus, London, 1965; reissued by Vintage and with additional material in 1994). A pioneering study which offers intelligent, accessible and discerning criticism, displaying a deep and serious understanding of the quality and character of Murdoch's work.

A. S. Byatt, 'People in Paper Houses: Attitudes to "Realism" and "Experiment" in English Postwar Fiction', in Malcolm Bradbury and David Palmer, eds., *The Contemporary English Novel* (Edward Arnold, London, 1971), pp. 19–41.

A. S. Byatt, *Iris Murdoch* (Longman and the British Council, Harlow, 1976).

A. S. Byatt, 'Contemporary Writers: Iris Murdoch' (Book Trust pamphlet published in conjunction with the British Council, 1988).

A. S. Byatt and Ignês Sodré, *Imagining Characters: In Conversation about Literature* (Chatto & Windus, London, 1995).

J-L. Chevalier, ed., *Rencontres avec Iris Murdoch* (Centre de Recherches de Litterature et Linguistique des Pays de Langue Anglaise, l'Université de Caen, 1978).

Peter J. Conradi, 'The Metaphysical Hostess', in *English Literary History*, XLVIII (Summer, 1981), pp. 427–53.

Peter J. Conradi, *The Saint and the Artist: A Study of the Fiction of Iris Murdoch* (Macmillan, Basingstoke, 1986; second edition, 1989). One of the most important and comprehensive critical works on Iris Murdoch in recent years. Includes useful and insightful chapters on all the major novels.

Peter J. Conradi, 'Iris Murdoch and Dostoevsky', in Richard Todd, ed., *Encounters with Iris Murdoch* (Free University Press, Amsterdam, 1987).

Peter J. Conradi, 'Platonism and Iris Murdoch', in A. Baldwin and S. Hutton, eds, *Platonism and the English Imagination* (Cambridge University Press, Cambridge, 1994), pp. 330–42.

Peter J. Conradi, 'Iris Murdoch and the Sea', in *Revue de la Societé d'études anglaises contemporaines*, no. 4 (June 1994).

Nirmal Datta, *Iris Murdoch: Freedom and Form* (Macmillan, New Delhi, 2000).

Douglas Brooks Davies, *Fielding, Dickens, Gosse, Murdoch and Oedipal Hamlet* (Macmillan, Basingstoke, 1989).

Elizabeth Dipple, *Iris Murdoch: Work for the Spirit* (Methuen, London, 1982).

Donna Gerstenberger, *Iris Murdoch* (Bucknell University Press, Lewisburg, 1975).

David J. Gordon, *Iris Murdoch's Fables of Unselfing* (Missouri, 1995).

Gabriele Griffin, *The Influence of Simone Weil on the Fiction of Iris Murdoch* (Mellen Research University Press, San Francisco, 1993).

Angela Hague, *Iris Murdoch's Comic Vision* (Susquehana University Press, Selinsgrove, 1984).

Barbara Hardy, *Tellers and Listeners* (Athlone Press, London, 1975).

Barbara Stevens Hensel, *Iris Murdoch's Paradoxical Novels: Thirty Years of Critical Reception* (Camden House, Boydell, Brown, Rochester, New York, 2001). On Murdoch's many roles as a philosophical novelist, as a thinker on psychological morality and as a postmodernist experimenter.

Deborah Johnson, *Iris Murdoch* (in the Key Women Writers series, The Harvester Press, Brighton, 1987).

Richard C. Kane, *Iris Murdoch, Muriel Spark and John Fowles: Didactic Demons in Modern Fiction* (Fairleigh Dickinson Press, Rutherford, 1988).

Leonard Kriegel, 'Iris Murdoch: Everybody Through the Looking Glass', in Charles Shapiro, ed., *Contemporary British Novelists* (South Illinois University Press, Carbondale, 1965).

Darlene D. Mettler, *Sound and Sense: Musical Allusion and Imagery in the Novels of Iris Murdoch* (Peter Lang, New York, 1991).

Modern Fiction Studies, special Iris Murdoch issue, XV, 3 (1969).

Bran Nicol, *Iris Murdoch: The Retrospective Vision* (Palgrave, Basingstoke, 1999).

Bran Nicol, *Iris Murdoch for Beginners* (Writers and Readers, London, 2001).

Patrick J. O'Connor, *To Love the Good: The Moral Philosophy of Iris Murdoch* (Peter Lang, New York, 1996).

Diana Phillips, *Agencies of the Good in the Work of Iris Murdoch* (Peter Lang, Frankfurt am Main, 1991).

Rubin Rabinowitz, 'Iris Murdoch', in G. Stade, ed., *Six Contemporary British Novelists* (Colombia University Press, New York, 1976).

Sugana Ramanathan, *Iris Murdoch: Figures of Good* (London, 1990).

Anne Rowe, *Salvation by Art: The Visual Arts and the Novels of Iris Murdoch* (Edwin Mellen Press, Lampeter, 2001). A particularly helpful work of criticism, giving the importance of setting and the visual in Murdoch's life and work.

Lorna Sage, 'Female Fictions', in *The Contemporary English Novel*, Malcolm Bradbury and David Palmer, eds (Edward Arnold, London, 1979), pp. 67–87.

Lorna Sage, *Women in the House of Fiction* (Macmillan, London, 1992).

Jacques Sauvage, 'Symbol as Narrative Device: An Interpretation of Iris Murdoch's *The Bell*', in *English Studies*, XXXXIII, no. 2 (April 1962), pp. 81–96.

Robert Scholes, *Fabulation and Metafiction* (University of Illinois Press, Urbana and London, 1978), pp. 56–74.

Carol Seiler-Franklin, *Boulder pushers: Women in the Fiction of Margaret Drabble, Doris Lessing and Iris Murdoch* (Peter Lang, Bern, 1979).

Hilda Spear, *Iris Murdoch* (Macmillan, London, 1995).

Richard Todd, 'The Plausibility of *The Black Prince*', *Dutch Quarterly*, vol. 2 (1978), pp. 82–93.

Richard Todd, *Iris Murdoch: The Shakespearian Interest* (Vision Press, London and New York, 1979).

Richard Todd, *Iris Murdoch* (London and New York, 1984).

Richard Todd, *Encounters with Iris Murdoch* (Free University Press, Amsterdam, 1988).

Lindsey Tucker, ed., *Critical Essays on Iris Murdoch* (G. K. Hall, Boston, Mass., 1987).

Peter Wolfe, *The Disciplined Heart: Iris Murdoch and her Novels* (University of Missouri Press, Columbia, 1966).

NEWSLETTER

The *Iris Murdoch Newsletter* is published by the Iris Murdoch Society. It began publishing in July 1987. Contact Dr Anne Rowe, 21 Upper Park Road, Kingston-upon-Thames, Surrey KT2 5LB, or Tony Bove, 5400 W. Autumn Springs Court, Muncie, Indiana 47304, USA.

The editors

Jonathan Noakes has taught English in secondary schools in Britain and Australia for fifteen years. For six years he ran A-level English studies at Eton College where he is a housemaster.

Margaret Reynolds is Reader in English at Queen Mary, University of London, and the presenter of BBC Radio 4's *Adventures in Poetry*. Her publications include *The Sappho Companion* and (with Angela Leighton) *Victorian Women Poets*. Her most recent book is *The Sappho History*.

Louisa Joyner completed her PhD at the University of London. She is an editor and critic.

ALSO AVAILABLE IN VINTAGE LIVING TEXTS

❑	*American Fiction*	0099445069	£5.99
❑	*Martin Amis*	0099437651	£6.99
❑	*Margaret Atwood*	009943704X	£6.99
❑	*Louis de Bernières*	0099437570	£6.99
❑	*A. S. Byatt*	0099452219	£5.99
❑	*Roddy Doyle*	0099452197	£5.99
❑	*Sebastian Faulks*	0099437562	£6.99
❑	*John Fowles*	0099460882	£5.99
❑	*Susan Hill*	0099452189	£5.99
❑	*Ian McEwan*	0099437554	£6.99
❑	*Toni Morrison*	009943766X	£6.99
❑	*Salman Rushdie*	0099437643	£6.99
❑	*Jeanette Winterson*	0099437678	£6.99

- All Vintage books are available through mail order or from your local bookshop.
- Payment may be made using Access, Visa, Mastercard, Diners Club, Switch and Amex, or cheque, eurocheque and postal order (sterling only).

❑❑❑❑❑❑❑❑❑❑❑❑❑❑❑❑

Expiry Date:_____ Signature:_____

Please allow £2.50 for post and packing for the first book and £1.00 per book thereafter.

ALL ORDERS TO:
Vintage Books, Books by Post, TBS Limited, The Book Service,
Colchester Road, Frating Green, Colchester, Essex, CO7 7DW, UK.
Telephone: (01206) 256 000
Fax: (01206) 255 914

NAME: _____

ADDRESS:_____

_____

_____

Please allow 28 days for delivery. Please tick box if you do not wish to
receive any additional information.
Prices and availability subject to change without notice.   ❑